D1624683

The
WISDOM
of
THE CONFUCIANS

The
WISDOM
of
THE CONFUCIANS

Compiled by
Zhou Xun with T.H. Barrett

ONEWORLD
OXFORD

THE WISDOM OF THE CONFUCIANS

Oneworld Publications
(Sales and Editorial)
185 Banbury Road
Oxford OX2 7AR
England
www.oneworld-publications.com

© Oneworld 2001

ISBN 1–85168–259–7

Cover and text design by Design Deluxe
Typeset by Cyclops Media Productions
Printed and bound by Graphicom Srl, Vicenza, Italy

CONTENTS

ACKNOWLEDGEMENTS

The publisher would like to thank Evelyn Nagai Berthrong for supplying the colour photographs that appear throughout the book. The line drawings that appear on pages xvi, 20, 56, 63, 75, 87, 108, 120, 131, 132, 155, 160, 172, 189 and 191 are taken from 'The Mustard Seed Garden manual of painting' by Chieh Tzu Yuan Hua Chuan.

Statue of Confucius at entry to the new Confucian Institute, Qufu.

INTRODUCTION

Little anthologies of wisdom are very much in vogue today, but in the Confucian tradition at least they have a long history as well. The first book translated from Chinese into a European language in the late sixteenth century was just such an anthology of Confucian derivation, an anthology which was popular from Korea to Vietnam. Both the major figures in the Chinese Confucianism of the past millennium produced anthologies in order to put their views across. Even the sayings of Confucius may be thought of as an anthology, since in the estimation of modern scholarship only a part of the *Analects of Confucius* reports the actual words of the master himself, while many more probably derive from words put into his mouth by later disciples.

And in a sense this is entirely fitting, for Confucius himself claimed no special revelation. Rather, he was simply trying to preserve the best of the cultural tradition in which he had been brought up, in the middle of an era of increasing change. Cultural traditions, of course, may be affected by the contributions of individuals, but they can only survive if a substantial group of people is prepared to sustain and support them. No die-hard conservative, Confucius accepted that changes and losses were inevitable, and that it was for example no longer possible to know much about the heroic rulers who had contributed so much to society in the distant past. But he did feel that through careful education a worthwhile wisdom could be transmitted to the future, and his optimism has been justified by the durability of his teachings.

At first his followers, with their fondness for ancient poems and half-forgotten rituals, probably seemed far too antiquarian in their interests for the generals and utterly pragmatic chief ministers who held sway in the climactic battles between heavily militarised states which presaged the eventual unification of China in 221 BCE. But the totalitarian regime of the First Emperor proved so harsh that it was swept away soon after his death by mass rebellions. Succeeding rulers seem to have recognised that in the absence of a strong fear of one's enemies, the only thing that would hold a vast empire together had to be the values enshrined in a common cultural tradition. Though Confucius seems to have been virtually ignored by rulers in his lifetime, his teachings were eventually taken up by the state.

The results were mixed. Early Confucians, while keen to advise rulers, had been as clear about the moral autonomy of the individual as any early Western thinker. But they expected society to be hierarchical, and so when the state decided to sponsor Confucian studies, they found themselves under heavy pressure to conform, to put loyalty to the emperor above all else. Confucianism was not and indeed is not the only way of thinking that those in authority have tried to interpret as simply knowing one's place. And Confucianism did not end up so closely linked to the Chinese empire that when the state collapsed it was thrown into complete discredit. Instead, from the third century CE onwards it was restricted for many centuries largely to its core role of providing a cultural heritage that was acquired through education.

During this time, as the Chinese slowly struggled to rebuild their lost unity, many put their trust in other, more private, hopes found in religions like Buddhism or Daoism. But once the empire was reunited, both these great religious traditions in the long run failed to develop a relationship with the Chinese state capable of sustaining its collective endeavours as effectively as they nourished the individual spiritual aspirations of its subjects. The practical wisdom imparted by a Confucian education – and especially wisdom about the process of learning itself – proved of enduring value to those entering the imperial civil service. What Confucianism appeared to lack was any spiritual dimension comparable to the religious prescriptions of its rivals. But despite the clear reluctance of Confucius himself to devote time to religious questions, the appreciation of the human condition even in early

Confucianism left room for the development of some ideas on this topic. From about 800 CE onwards, and especially during the eleventh century, a group of thinkers known as Neo-Confucians gradually evolved a worldview that allowed an individual to follow personal goals of self-development as well as social goals as a useful member of society.

It was this new dual vision of the transformation of self and society that now spread throughout East Asia. This was made easier because the region had already become familiar with the basic texts of early Confucianism, thanks to the earlier spread of Chinese literacy. And for centuries, even more than with Latin in Western Europe, there was no other form of literacy available, so Chinese, Vietnamese, Korean and Japanese scholars could all read what the Neo-Confucians wrote. Of course they responded at different times and in different ways. The overall pattern in regard to Vietnam is as yet unclear, but it is notable, for example, that the Koreans, once they had emerged from a period of Mongol domination at the start of the fourteenth century, took over the Chinese Neo-Confucianism of the era and applied it to their own society without ever, as it were, looking back.

One result of this single-mindedness was that when fresh currents emerged in Chinese Confucianism in the fifteenth century, the Koreans tended to look askance at these novelties.

Roof tiles and finials, Forest of Confucius, Qufu.

This was very different from the pattern of acceptance in Japan, which had to wait in any case until the seventeenth century, when the warfare of Japan's medieval period gave way to an era of peace. Confucianism, with its interest in the arts of civil government, attracted a measure of state support, but Japanese attitudes to Neo-Confucianism were pragmatic and critical. In retrospect many scholars have seen this period of intense debate as one of preparation for Japan's remarkable transformation into a modern power during the late nineteenth and early twentieth centuries. By contrast, however, during much of the early twentieth century Confucianism was seen as a barrier to progress in China.

It is undoubtedly true that not only Confucius but also most of his followers in East Asia took a more conservative stance than became popular in the twentieth century over such matters as the status of women. But the tradition's emphasis on other matters, such as the importance of education, by the end of the twentieth century came to be seen as much more beneficial to social and economic progress. The emerging economic strength of societies such as Taiwan or Singapore seemed to point to positive elements in the Confucian heritage, so that some even argued that a strong regard for hierarchy must be one ingredient in economic success. How such issues will look in the light of the twenty-first century is still impossible to judge. Our purpose in this historical sketch has not in any case been to trace the evolution of Confucianism as such, but simply to point out that many diverse societies in many different times and places have found something of value within the tradition.

It is for this reason that we have tried to cast our net quite widely in compiling this anthology, concentrating not simply on basic Confucianism but also ranging across time and space to provide a variety of examples of Confucian wisdom. For this was a tradition which was broad enough to appeal to different people in different ways. To some it offered a means of self-improvement, of high ethical standards and the methods necessary to achieve them. To others it offered more immediate, practical advice on how to get an education, and get along with friends and especially family. To yet others it offered a vision of the complete transformation of society, perhaps of the whole world. Different facets of Confucian wisdom no doubt appealed to the same people at different times in their lives.

Here we are able to provide just a taste of the riches of this great tradition, though we have also tried to convey an understanding of it as well. For rather than throw disconnected sayings at the reader, so as to create a parody of Confucius as a purveyor of inscrutable platitudes, we have taken great care to set all the most basic information within a clear interpretative framework. Here and in the related translations, however, our guide has been the contemporary understanding of the tradition amongst those who were educated in it: this, we hope, will provide immediately useful insight, rather than a historical reconstruction of Confucian thought. In order to give the reader an opportunity to explore yet further, we have provided not only a brief account of the sources that we have used in compiling this anthology but also some suggestions for further general reading.

THE FAMILY

In China, the family is held in the highest esteem. It was central to Confucian thought, and was regarded as the most fundamental unit of any society:

T HERE IS a common saying: 'The empire, the state, the family.' The root of the empire is in the state. The root of the state is in the family.

Mencius 4A:5

Perceived as a co-operative unit, the family in Confucian tradition was represented as an intrinsic part of a state and society. According to Zhang Zai (1020–77), an eleventh century Neo-Confucian scholar, the universe was in fact one family. Public morality was understood to be based on Ren, benevolence or humanity, the principle of love. This was a natural and humanistic love. It was regarded as a universal virtue and was considered to be the supreme virtue amongst the Five Constant Virtues – humanity, righteousness, propriety, wisdom and faithfulness. As the natural world is formed by continuous interactions between the Five Phases – wood, metal, fire, water and earth – so the Five Constant Virtues were viewed as the basis of a well-functioning and ordered society.

The virtue of humanity was understood to have come from feelings of love. Such feelings needed to be cultivated and it was participation in family life that first endowed individuals with such feelings. Thus, children of a good household should learn the feelings of love by first loving their parents and, in order to receive love and affection from the children, parents must first demonstrate that love. In other words, mutual love and respect is seen as the cornerstone of the family system. According to the Confucian Classics, there are five kinds of basic human relationships: those between parents and children, between husband and wife, between older brother and younger brother, between ruler and his subjects, and between friends:

> BETWEEN FATHER and son there should be affection.
> Between husband and wife there should be attention to their separate functions.
> Between old and young there should be proper order.
> Between ruler and minister there should be righteousness.
> Between friends there should be faithfulness.

Mencius 3A:4

To achieve an orderly family requires appropriate relationships between parents and children, husband and wife, and elder and younger brothers.

Imperial Vault of Heaven, Temple of Heaven, Beijing.

FILIAL PIETY

It is believed that

A YOUNG man's duty is to behave well to his parents at home and to his elders abroad.

Analects 1:6

To behave well towards one's parents is to be filial. Filial piety, or Xiao, was considered to be the most essential element in regulating the family. It was revered as the root of humanity and was regarded as the most stable foundation of all love:

F ILIAL PIETY and fraternal submission! Are they not the root of benevolent actions?

Analects 1:2

In Confucian tradition, filial piety takes many forms. Originally, it was often used to refer to one's piety towards the spirits of one's ancestors. Since the fourth century, the meaning of Xiao *has increasingly extended to one's piety, or feelings, towards one's living parents. According to* The Classic of Filial Piety *(post third century), the ultimate filial piety meant total obedience towards the Son of Heaven or the emperor, whereas, within the family,* Xiao *is manifested by obeying and supporting one's parents. However, Confucius taught this should be more than just mere material support to one's parents:*

NOWADAYS, FILIAL piety means to make sure that one's parents have enough to eat. But dogs and horses are also cared for to the same extent. If there is no feeling of respect, what is the difference?

Analects 2:7

FILIAL PIETY does not consist merely in young people undertaking the hard work, when there are things that need to be done, or serving their elders first with wine and food. It is much more than that.

Analects 2:8

For Mencius,

THE MAN of great filial piety, to the end of his life, has his desire toward his parents.

Mencius 5A:1

In other words, a man who never forgets his origins, who is continually loving and concerned about his parents to the end of his life, may be called a man of great filial piety. A good example was Shun, a legendary emperor of ancient China:

SHUN WAS indeed perfectly filial! Even when he was fifty, he was full of longing desire about his parents.

Mencius 6B:3

By having such a great virtue, it was believed that one (Shun):

COULD NOT but have obtained the throne, great riches and his fame, and that he was able to attain his long life … Was not Shun a man of great filial piety? His virtue was that of a sage: his dignity was the throne; his riches were all within the four seas. After his death his spirit received sacrifice

Formal entry to dwelling, Forest of Confucius, Qufu.

in the ancestral temple, and his descendants preserved the sacrifice to him for long generations.

Doctrine of the Mean, chapter 16

Furthermore, to obey one's parents should not mean passive obedience. Children were said to have responsibilities towards their parents:

IN SERVING father and mother, one remonstrates gently. If one sees that they are intent on not following advice, one continues to be respectful and does not show disobedience; and even if one finds it burdensome, one does not feel resentful.

Analects 4:18

According to Mencius, commonly there are five things that may be considered unfilial:

FIRSTLY, PHYSICAL laziness in attending to the nourishment of one's parents is considered unfilial.

Secondly, addiction to gambling, playing and drinking, and having no time to attend to the nourishment of one's parents is considered unfilial.

Thirdly, obsession with material things, money and one's own wife and children without attending to the nourishment of one's parents is considered unfilial.

Fourthly, following one's own desires so as to bring disgrace to one's parents is considered unfilial.

Fifthly, being too courageous, loving to fight and to quarrel so that one might bring danger to one's parents is considered unfilial.

Mencius 4B:30

THEREFORE, IT is thought, when the parents are still alive,
One should not only love but also show reverence towards them.
One should support them both materially and spiritually.
One should avoid bringing humiliation or harm to one's parents by one's bad behaviour. One should remonstrate with gentleness towards one's parents even in dispute.
One should also keep in good health, for:
It is our illness that causes our fathers and mothers to worry.

Analects 2:6

In addition, it was taught that:

WHEN FATHER and mother are alive, one does not travel far; and if one does travel, one must have a fixed destination.

Analects 4:19

Although the word Xiao *has been taken to mean, and is also commonly understood as, filial piety towards one's living parents, in Confucian tradition the teaching of piety towards the spirits of ancestors or dead parents continued to play an important part. According to Confucius, it was through the practice of* Li, *rites, rituals, ceremonies, good deeds and so on, that one may obtain the self-realisation of* Ren:

GOOD IS the one who submits himself to ritual.

Analects 12:1

Scholar's pavilion, birthplace of Mencius, Zou, Shandong Province.

Thus it is taught:

W HEN THE father is alive, you observe a man's intentions. It is when the father is dead that you observe the man's actions. If for three years he makes no change from the ways of his father, he is called filial.

Analects 1:11

It is therefore considered proper that, following the death of one's parents, one must continue to show solicitude for them 'with sacrifices so that their virtue will be restored to fullness' (Analects 1:9). The performance of funeral rites after the death of one's parents was called 'the great thing' by Mencius:

T HE NOURISHMENT of parents when living is not sufficient to be accounted the great thing. It is only in the performance of obsequies when dead that we have what can be considered the great thing.

Mencius 6B:13

IN DISCHARGING the funeral duties to parents, men indeed are constrained to do their utmost.

Mencius 3A:2

The practice of funeral rites goes back to very early China:

THE PRACTICE of the rites in harmony is regarded as the most valuable thing, and in the ways of the ancient kings this is regarded as the most beautiful thing.

Analects 1:12

It was, according to Confucius himself, the highest form of filial piety:

FILIAL PIETY is seen in those who carry out the wishes of their forefathers and carry forward their undertakings skilfully.

Doctrine of the Mean, chapter 18

Papier-mâché figures of sacrificial animals at a ceremony loosely based on Confucian ritual descriptions. Performers wear Manchu dress. Confucian Temple, Qufu.

IN SPRING and autumn, they repaired and beautified the temple halls of their forefathers, set forth their ancestral vessels,

Displayed their various robes and presented the offerings of the several seasons.

By means of the ceremonies of the ancestral temple, they distinguished the royal kindred according to their order of descent.

By ordering the parties according to their rank, they distinguished the more noble and the less.

By the arrangement of the services, they made a distinction of talents and worth.

In the ceremony of general pledging, the inferiors presented their cups to their superiors.

And thus something was given the lowest to do.

At the concluding feast, places were given according to the whiteness of the hair, and thus made the distinction of years.

They occupied the places of their forefathers,
practised their ceremonies and performed their music.
They reverenced those whom they honoured
and loved those whom they regarded with affection.
Thus they served the dead as they would have served
  them alive;
they served the departed as they would have served them
  had they been continued among them.
This was the highest display of filial piety.

Doctrine of the Mean, chapter 18

B Y THE ceremonies of the sacrifices to Heaven and Earth they served God, and by the ceremonies of the ancestral temple they sacrificed to their ancestors. He who understands the ceremonies of the sacrifices to Heaven and Earth and the meaning of the several sacrifices to ancestors would find the government of a State as easy as to look into his palm.

Doctrine of the Mean, chapter 18

HUSBANDS AND WIVES

While filial piety was considered to be the most stable foundation of all human love, it is often understood that the relationship between husbands and wives reflects the beginnings of all human relationships:

> THE WAY, *Dao*, of the superior man begins with the relations between husband and wife;
> But at its utmost, it reaches as far as heavens and earth.

> *Doctrine of the Mean, chapter 11*

It is therefore not surprising that within Confucian tradition Heaven was sometimes represented as the father and Earth as the mother.

> HEAVEN IS my father and Earth is my mother,
> And even a small creature such as me finds an intimate place amongst their midst.

> ZHANG ZAI, *The Western Inscription*

In Confucian tradition, royal marriage was often exalted:

> A ROYAL marriage means the union of two ruling houses
> For the purpose of carrying on the royal lineage and
> Producing offspring to preside over the worship of
>   Heaven and Earth,
> Of the ancestral spirits, and of the gods of land and
>   grains.
>
> If Heaven and Earth do not come together, there is no life
>   in this world.
> A royal marriage has the purpose of perpetuating the
>   ruling house
> For thousands of generations.

Book of Rites, chapter 24

As the natural world is generated by the cosmic force of Yin Yang, the interaction between, or the mutual support and respect of, husband and wife was said to have laid the foundation for the continuation of human life, and affection and love between all mankind:

Confucian statuary, birthplace of Mencius.

THE CEREMONY of royal marriage is the ultimate symbol of respect, and as it is the ultimate symbol of respect,

The king goes with its crown to welcome the princess from her own home personally

Because he regards the bride as so close in relationship to him.

He goes personally because the relationship is regarded as personal.

Therefore the sovereign cultivates the sense of respect and personal relationship.

To neglect to show respect is to disregard the personal relationship.

Without love, there will be no personal relationship.

So love and respect are the foundation of government.

Book of Rites, chapter 24

The union of husband and wife was also highly praised by Mencius:

THAT MALE and female shall dwell together is the greatest of all human relationships.

Mencius 5A:2

Desire for each other was regarded as a natural stage of their lives for both the male and female:

> THE CHILD'S desire is towards his father and mother.
> When he becomes conscious of being attracted by beauty,
> His desire is towards a young and beautiful woman.
> When he has a wife and children, his desire is towards them.

Mencius 5A:1

Within the union of husband and wife, it was thought just as Yang was represented as the active force and Yin as the tranquil force, husband and wife were understood to have different roles within a family.

THE HUSBAND and wife should have different duties.

Book of Rites, chapter 24

They should 'attend to their separate functions' (Mencius 3A:4). This is sometimes referred to as 'discriminating love'. It should not however be taken to mean an unequal relationship, or a subordinate relationship, between husband and wife, but rather a complementary relationship. In other words, the husband should treat the wife as a female, who is Yin in nature, whereas the wife should treat the husband as a male, who is Yang in nature. Without the help and support of the one, the other is incomplete. Such a relationship should also be reciprocal; the husband should treat the wife as a wife, respect her role as a wife, not as a sister or as any other female and vice versa:

THE ANCIENT great kings always showed respect or proper consideration to their wives and children in accordance with proper principle. How can one be disrespectful toward one's wife since she is the centre of the home?

Book of Rites, chapter 24

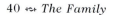

An acolyte or guardian on a terrace in the Forest of Confucius, Qufu.

Husband and wife should also care for and love each other in the way that each would wish from the other. When Yin Yang reaches balance, it brings Great Harmony. The harmony between husband and wife is a manifestation of their love and it may be attained through Li. A harmonious relationship between a husband and wife was regarded as the basis of a stable family. It was therefore regarded as essential for husband and wife to exercise care for each other, to maintain harmony within the family. Marriage itself is a promise of the Great Harmony.

IT IS WRITTEN in the *Book of Songs*,
Look at that peach tree, so fresh and pretty!
How green and thick are its leaves!
The girl is going to her husband's house,
And there she will live in harmony with the people of her
    husband's home.

Great Learning, chapter 8

When there is harmony at home, their family life will be blessed:

> IT IS WRITTEN in the *Book of Songs*,
> Happy union with wife and children is like the music of
>   lute and harp.
> When brothers live in concord and at peace,
> The harmony is delightful and will not cease.
> Such a happy union is like a lamp that lights at home
> And you shall enjoy the pleasure of your wife and
>   children.

Doctrine of the Mean, chapter 14

Ironically, however, Confucius's own eccentric, almost crazy, behaviour was thought to be the main thing that exasperated his wife and caused her to run away. Divorce also seems to have been the tradition amongst his immediately succeeding family generations and his disciples.

BROTHERLY LOVE

To maintain a harmonious family involves more than just husband and wife; it also concerns brothers and children. It was taught that in order to cultivate Ren, *while one must demonstrate filial piety,* Xiao, *towards one's parents, one must also develop* Di, *brotherly love and respect:*

BY LEARNING to respect one's elder brother, one was preparing to serve all the elders of the country.

Great Learning, chapter 8

Gentility in the elder brother and respect in the younger were considered to be one of the human duties, as well as being human nature:

A YOUNGER brother walks slowly and follows after his elders. If he hurried and stepped in front of them we would say he was not a proper younger brother. It would not be a matter of his being incapable of walking slowly, but of his failing to do so.

Mencius 6B:2

Statue of Confucius at entry to the new Confucian Institute, Qufu.

It was taught by Mencius that while one may develop the virtue of humanity by serving one's parents, one attains the virtue of righteousness by learning the appropriate relationship with one's brothers, and from humanity and righteousness all other virtues grew:

THE MOST precious jewel of Humanity is in serving one's parents. The most precious jewel of Righteousness is in obedience to elder brothers. The most precious jewel of Wisdom is to know these two and to follow them consistently. The most precious jewel of Ritual is in setting the two into a pattern and bringing them into practice. It is also out of these two things that the most precious and joyous music flows. It is in pleasure they grow, and growing they are irrepressible. And being irrepressible all unknowingly the feet take up the measure and hands begin the dance.

Mencius 4A:27

Therefore by learning to respect one's elder brother and serving one's parents, a person may develop those essential qualities as a ruler of the state.

IT IS WRITTEN in the *Book of Songs*:
The gentlemen of the country treated their elder
 brothers properly.
They also treated their younger brothers properly.
Only by living in harmony with one's elder and younger
 brother
Is a ruler then ready to serve as a model for the country.

Great Learning, chapter 8

Yet, according to Mencius, the origin of righteousness was internal: one develops the virtue of righteousness within one's family.

ONLY BY respecting one's elder brother may one learn to respect the elders of others.

Mencius 6A:5

CHILDREN

To maintain the Great Harmony at home, parents must show and teach their children kindness. Kindness was regarded as an aspect of humanity, Ren, *or a manifestation of love, in Confucian teachings. Kindness towards children was said to be natural in every parent.*

PARENTS IN caring for their children do more than what is required. Such is not a learnt skill, just as a girl need not learn to nurse a baby before her marriage.

Great Learning, chapter 8

It was therefore considered to be against human nature to be unkind towards children. Yet being kind towards one's children should not be taken to mean blind love. Parents must not lose their sense of judgement towards their loved ones:

Roof tiles and finials, Forest of Confucius, Qufu.

P EOPLE DO not know the faults of their children as they cannot know the imperceptible growth of the rice plants in their fields.

Great Learning, chapter 7

So to love one's children meant to teach them to learn to cultivate their hearts from a very early stage so that they would grow up to know kindness. By teaching kindness to children, they learn to love their parents and brothers and to show respect to their seniors. Thus it was taught that:

B Y TEACHING kindness, parents are training [the child] for the role of ruler.

Great Learning, chapter 8

In other words, just as by learning filial piety one is training to serve the ruler of the state and by learning to respect elder brothers one is training to serve all the elders of the country, by learning kindness the child is training to become a kind person.

FAMILY AND SOCIETY

Kindness is essential in maintaining the harmony within family and society. Therefore, parental kindness and fraternal love, together with filial piety, were regarded in Confucian tradition as the main principles in regulating the family. Even so, according to Confucian teaching, the word Shu, reciprocity, the golden rule of conducting one's personal life, was also the golden rule in conducting family relationships:

D O NOT do unto others the things you do not want others to do unto yourself.

Analects 15:24

This rule of reciprocity was also regarded as one's moral duty towards society:

T O SERVE my sovereign as I would expect a minister under me to serve me. To behave towards friends as I would expect them to behave towards me.

Great Learning, chapter 8

And it was taught:

> BY LIVING in harmony with people in one's home, one is able to set an example to the people of the nation.
> As it is written in the *Book of Songs*,
> When the prince is righteous
> He sets a country in order.
> Because he himself served as a worthy example as a father, son, and elder brother and as a younger brother,
> Therefore the people took him for their model.

Great Learning, chapter 8

In other words, when goodwill prevails in one family, it influences the whole society; on the other hand, one man's evil may bring ultimate destruction: this was an essential element in Confucian teachings:

FROM THE loving example of one family a whole State becomes loving, and from its courtesies the whole State becomes courteous, while from the ambition and

Imperial Vault of Heaven, Temple of Heaven, Beijing.

perverseness of one man the whole State may be led to rebellion and disorder; such is the nature of influence.

Great Learning, chapter 9

It is an ordered and well-run household that is the basis of a strong state:

> THOSE WHO wished to manifest bright virtue throughout all under Heaven first brought order to their states.
> Those who wished to bring order to their states first regulated their family.

Great Learning, chapter 4

To bring order to the state, it was considered essential for the ruler to treat the multitude with kindness and deal with the masses as his children. As Mencius taught:

THE WAY to win an empire is to win the people first. The way to win the people is to win their heart: simply to gather what they like and not to burden them with what they dislike.

The people turn to a loving ruler as water flows downwards and as wild beasts fly to the wilderness.

Mencius 4A:10

In other words, a good ruler must show kindness to his people as a parent to his children. In return the people would show their piety towards the ruler. Therefore in traditional China, the rulers and officials were often referred to as the 'father mother officials', or as 'parents of the people'.

> AS IT WAS written in the *Book of Songs*
> How pleased are the people with their ruler
> For he is like a parent to them.
> The ruler loves what the common people love
> And hates what the common people hate.
> That is how to be a parent to the common people.

Great Learning, chapter 9

WHEN THOSE in authority are respectful toward the old
   people,
Then the common people learn to be good sons.
When those in authority show respect to their superiors,
Then the common people learn respect and humility.
When those in authority show kindness to the young and
   helpless,
The common people do not follow the opposite course.

Great Learning, chapter 9

*Only then would there be moral order, peace and prosperity
for the whole country – the realisation of* Zhong, *or the Mean,
and* He, *or the Great Harmony.*

SOCIETY

CENTRALITY AND GREAT HARMONY

Such was the Confucian ideal of a perfect society:

> CENTRALITY IS the foundation of the world.
> Great Harmony is the universal path of the world.
> When there is the realisation of Centrality and Great
>   Harmony,
> All Heaven and Earth is in proper order
> Then all things will grow into fullness.

Doctrine of the Mean, chapter 1

But what did Centrality and Great Harmony mean? It is taught:

WHEN PASSIONS, such as joy, anger, grief and pleasure, have not been aroused, or are unexpressed, one is in the state of Centrality. When they are expressed appropriately, one has reached the Great Harmony.

Doctrine of the Mean, chapter 1

In other words, before feelings are aroused or expressed, they are in what is called their natural state, neither partial nor inclining to one side. When feelings are expressed the way they should be expressed, when one feels pleasure as one should, when one expresses anger as one should, and so on, one is following the way of nature. The way of nature is Centrality, the way of nature is the foundation of the world. By following the way of nature one reaches the Great Harmony. In Confucian tradition, nature is understood as the 'Way of Heaven'. As the Neo-Confucian scholar Cheng Yi (1033–1107) put it:

WHAT IS endowed by Heaven is destiny and what is received by man is called nature.

YI ZHUAN, *Commentary on the Book of Changes 1:2b* in Graham, *Two Chinese Philosophers*

According to Mencius,

TO KNOW one's nature is to know Heaven.

Mencius 7A:1

DAO

The concept of Heaven as the ultimate power which controls events in history, the prospects of society and human affairs in general was derived from The Spring and Autumn Annals *(fifth century* BCE*). It was considered to be Confucius's own work, and its importance was fully confirmed largely due to the effort of the Han Confucian scholar/politician Dong Zhongshu (195–115* BCE*). Dong was responsible for establishing Confucianism as the theoretical foundation of the imperfect imperial state during the Han Dynasty (206* BCE*–220* CE*). According to Dong, human life and society are subject to universal laws instituted by Heaven. Humanity is Heaven's means to extend and to maintain order in the world. Heaven endows the ruler with responsibilities in governing the world. Regular and irregular natural events all have symbolic politico-cosmic meanings.*

Although in the Confucian tradition, Heaven was recognised as being high and brilliant, it did not merely mean a supernatural force. The object of knowledge of Heaven was to know man. Heaven was often spoken of in terms of Principle, the Way or Dao. For earlier Confucian sages, such as the great master himself and Mencius, Dao was less of an abstract concept than has sometimes been thought. When they talked with people about Dao, they often did so from the view of daily human affairs:

> THE WAY lies in what is near, yet men seek for it in what is remote.
> The work lies in what is easy, yet men seek for it in what is difficult.
> If each man would love his parents and show respect to his elders,
> There would be peace under Heaven.

Mencius 4A:11

> BY FULFILLING one's duty towards those who are near
> One learns to regulate one's personal conduct and character.
> But in order to learn about one's duties towards those who are near to him
> One must understand the nature and order of human society.
> In order to understand the nature and order of human society
> One must know the Heaven.

Doctrine of the Mean, chapter 11

Therefore, the knowledge of Heaven, as taught in the Confucian tradition, is made known to man through human conduct and affairs:

> HEAVEN DOES not speak.
> It simply shows its will through personal conduct and
>   human affairs …
> Thus, it says:
> Heaven sees what the people see;
> Heaven hears what the people hear.

Mencius 5A:5

In the Confucian tradition, Heaven was the ultimate source of the universe and it was thought to be responsible for the creation of all things in the natural world:

> IT IS WRITTEN in the *Book of Songs*,
> 'Heaven produced mankind
> And gave them all things, and rules in guarding the
>   world.'

Mencius 6A:6

As the creator of all things, Heaven also regulates all things:

> THUS HEAVEN produced things,
> According to their varied qualities
> If any needed to be planted and nourished
> So it would be done.
> If any needed to be discarded and thrown away
> So it would be done.

Doctrine of the Mean, chapter 16

Formal entry to dwelling, Forest of Confucius, Qufu.

LI

Human society, as part of Heaven's creation, was endowed with heavenly order. Li, the principle of social order, was said to be a great channel through which human beings follow the orders, or laws, of Heaven and direct within their proper courses the expressions of the human heart. In Confucian teachings Li practically covered the entire social, moral and religious structure of ancient Chinese society:

L I IS BASED on heaven and patterned on the earth. It deals with the worship of the spirits and is extended to the rites and ceremonies of funerals, sacrifices to ancestors, archery, carriage driving, coming of age ceremonies [similar to the Bar Mitzvah in Jewish tradition], marriage, and court audiences or exchanges of diplomatic visits. Therefore the Teachers should show people the principle of a proper social order and through it everything becomes right in the family, the state and the world.

Book of Rites, chapter 7

Clearly in Confucian thought Li represented social norms. It was the principle aimed at restoring the ancient feudal order, with a clear hierarchy of ranks. Yet this principle of social order also applied to essential human relationships in family, social and political life. It provided a moral basis for human society:

WHEN I enter a country, I can easily tell its culture. When people are gentle in spirit, kind and simple in heart, it shows the country is concerned with poetry. When people are generous and show a good disposition, it shows the country is concerned with music. When people are quiet and thoughtful and sharp in observing things, it shows the country is following the principle in the *Book of Changes*. When people are humble and respectful and frugal in their habits, it shows people are taught *Li*.

Book of Rites, chapter 23

I IS TO a country what scales are to weight and what the carpenter's ruler is to straightness, and what the measure and the compasses are to squares and circles. Therefore, when the scales are exact, one cannot be mistaken in respect to weight; when the ruler is properly laid, one cannot be mistaken in respect to straightness; when the measure and compasses are properly used, one cannot be mistaken in respect to the right angle and the circular line. And when the sovereign is familiar with *Li*, he cannot be deceived by cunning and crooked manipulations. Therefore, the one who respects and follows *Li* is the one who has principles, and the one who does not respect and follow *Li* is the one without principles.

Book of Rites, chapter 23

According to Confucius,

L I IS THE greatest of all things people live by.

Book of Rites, chapter 23

Without Li, we do not know how to conduct a proper worship of the spirits of the universe; or how to establish the proper status of the king and the ministers, the ruler and the ruled, and the senior and the juniors; or how to distinguish the different degrees of family relationships. Therefore a gentleman should hold Li in high regard, and 'proceed to teach its principles to the people and regulate the forms of social life' (Book of Rites, ch. 24).

Scholar's pavilion, birthplace of Mencius, Zou, Shandong Province.

LI IS THE principle by which the ancient kings embodied the laws of Heaven and regulated the expressions of human nature. Therefore he who has attained *Li* shall live, and he who has lost it shall die.

Book of Rites, chapter 7

Li *is understood to be*

THE PRINCIPLE of social order, which prevents moral and social chaos as a dam to prevent flood, [and] there is nothing better than *Li* to maintain the authority and the governing of people.

Book of Rites, chapter 27

IN THE art of government, *Li* comes first. It is the means by which we establish the forms of worship, enabling the ruler to appear before the spirits of Heaven and Earth bringing sacrifices. It is also the means by which we establish forms of intercourse at the court and a sense of piety or respect between ruler and people. It revives the social and political life from confusion or disgrace. *Li* is therefore the foundation of government.

Book of Rites, chapter 24

[THUS TO] govern a country without *Li* is like tilling a field without a plough.

Book of Rites, chapter 9

However, for Confucius and many of his followers, Li was not a matter of rigid rules, as it was often misrepresented or misunderstood. According to Confucius, Li was not something fixed forever. It should be subject to change according to situations:

IT IS KNOWN that when the Yin succeeded the Xia, they modified *Li*. It is also known that when the Zhou succeeded the Yin, they too modified *Li*. Hence, we can foretell that this will apply to the successor of the Zhou, even though we may not know when that will be.

Analects 2:23

YI

For Confucius and his followers, change was inevitable and necessary. A functional and ordered society must adapt to changes. Therefore there should not be a single Li for all occasions and all things. Yet within a state or a society, there must be a standard higher principle which should be based on Li. Such principle was called Yi. Yi has sometimes been translated as the principle of righteousness. Yet in Confucian teachings it was often used in a wider sense to mean the principle of moral reason or rationality:

A SUPERIOR PERSON is more concerned to discover *Yi* while a lesser person is more concerned with his pay.

Analects 4:16

Papier-mâché figures of sacrificial animals at a ceremony loosely based on Confucian ritual descriptions. Performers wear Manchu dress. Confucian Temple, Qufu.

It was believed that through the enforcement of Yi, a ruler might obtain the principle of governing. And 'only when the country is rightly governed, will there be peace under Heaven'. According to Confucian teachings, there were nine rules of governing a state:

ALL WHO govern a state must follow the nine common yet difficult rules: cultivate their personal life; honour the worthy; show affection to their own family; respect their ministers; be kind and considerate to all who are in office; treat the masses as their own children; encourage all professions; be friendly to people from afar; and care for the principalities of the various states.

By cultivating his personal life, the ruler may attain the Way and set the model for the country. By honouring the worthy, the ruler may avoid being misled and bad judgement. By showing affection to one's own family, the ruler may avoid resentment or grumbling amongst his parents, uncles and brothers. By showing respect to his ministers, the ruler may avoid making errors. By showing kindness and caring for those who are in office, the ruler may win great loyalty amongst them. By treating the masses as his own children, they are led to exhort one another to goodness. By encouraging all professions, his own resources are made sufficient. By showing friendliness towards people from afar, the ruler may win followers from all over. By caring for the principalities of various states, the ruler will win the world.

To cultivate one's personal life one must be righteous and pure, dress carefully, not to do anything which is inappropriate or against the principles. To encourage the worthy one must disregard any gossiping or conspiracy and keep away from the seduction of women and beauty, and treasure virtues instead of material things. To encourage the family one should respect their positions and shower them with gifts, share their likes and dislikes. To encourage the ministers one should appoint them with tasks according to their talents and be confident in what they do. To encourage gentlemen of the office, one must be loyal, truthful and generous. To encourage the people, there should be only a certain time of the year that people have to do their national service; the government should also set up a proper system for collecting tax and products, and make sure there is no heavy burden being forced upon people. To encourage the creativity of artisans, one should regularly check and inspect their works and projects, and distribute food and meat according to their effort. As to people from afar, one should see them off when they leave and welcome them when they come; reward those who are talented and be tolerant and compassionate towards those who are less competent. This way one may win the whole world. If there are any aristocratic families whose family lines are broken, help them to restore them; if there is any state in danger of being extinguished, help to revive it; bring justice to the country which is corrupt and strengthen the one which is weak. Change the government cabinet regularly and use the talented. When a Duke leaves or retires, send him off with a huge present; but while in office keep him in modest conditions. These are the Nine Rules of governing a state.

Doctrine of the Mean, chapter 19

LAWS

On a more practical level, Confucius taught that to sustain a government,

PEOPLE MUST first have sufficient food to eat; there must be a strong army; and people must have confidence in the ruler.

Analects 12:7

When asked to make a choice between the three, Confucius declared:

I WOULD GO without the army first ... I would rather go without sufficient food for the people. There have always been deaths in every generation since man lived, but a nation cannot exist without confidence in its ruler.

Analects 12:7

The practice of government, according to Confucius, should be based on virtue, which was attained through the practice of Li, not of punishment.

GUIDE THE people with regulations and control them by the threat of punishment, and people will only try to keep out of prison but will not have any sense of honour or shame. But guide people by virtue and cultivate them by *Li*, and people will know about honour and respect.

Analects 2:3

TO GOVERN a nation by means of virtue is like the Pole Star, which shines as the rest revolve around it.

Analects 2:1

Punishment indicates a lack of public morality and a need to correct people's behaviour:

IN ANCIENT times, punishment was rarely used but today it is highly prevalent. The reason for this is that in ancient times people were first taught rites; punishment only came second. Today, rites are not taught, people are restricted by means of punishment. That is why punishment is prevalent today. As it was written in the *Book of History*: 'Bo Yi gave the code of law to restrain people by using punishment.' This means people should first be taught rites, and afterwards punishment may be applied. Without rites, people have no sense of shame; punishment was used to correct it … The object of applying the punishment is to end the need for punishment.

When managing people by means of teaching them rites, it is like a charioteer using reins. When controlling people by means of punishment, it is like a charioteer using a whip. A superior charioteer can move the horse by just holding the reins in the opposite direction. But if a charioteer uses only the whip without reins, the horse loses its way … A superior charioteer of the past could hold the reins like holding silk robes while their horses moved gracefully as dancers. There was no need to use a whip. That was why the ancient kings considered rites to be far more important than punishment, and people followed their rules. Today too much importance is given to punishment, so society is violent and full of crimes.

Kongcongzi, chapter 4

However, this does not suggest that Confucians considered law and punishment unimportant. According to Confucius, punishment was necessary in correcting people's misbehaviour, but it must be based on rites:

IN THE custom of Wu Yue, male and female bathe together; they are not kept apart. People there like to harass each other. Their punishments are heavy yet unsuccessful, for they lack rites. In the Middle Kingdom, it is taught there should be a difference between inside and outside; male and female should dress appropriately according to their class and type. eople there are law abiding even though their punishment is light, because they have rites.

Kongcongzi, chapter 4

In Confucian teachings, the purpose of punishment should not be to punish, but to lead one to become virtuous:

IN ANCIENT times, those who knew the law always managed to keep the law afar. This is because they put rites first. Today, those who know the law do not pardon those who committed crime. This is rather lacking in compassion. But keeping away from the method of imprisonment is a long-term method of preventing crimes. Lack of compassion is very short sighted, but the long-term method will bring the real cure. It is written in the *Book of Documents*: 'strictly apply five punishments in order to fulfil the three virtues', which means by carefully following punishment one learns to be virtuous.

Kongcongzi, chapter 4

Confucian statuary, birthplace of Mencius.

MUSIC

Apart from rites and punishments, music was also given an important place in Confucian teachings. It is said that Confucius called himself the 'one who devotes himself to rites and music' (Kongcongzi, ch. 1). It was believed that the ancient kings guided the people's ideals and aspirations by means of Li and prevented immorality by means of punishments. They also established harmony by means of music:

WHEN ANCIENT Kings had accomplished successfully, they composed music. The more successful they were, the more harmonious their music was. When music was truly harmonious, Heaven and Earth reflected such harmony, so did all the animals. Kuei was Shun's music master. He had a real talent by means of music to bring the principle of governing into full realisation.

Kongcongzi, chapter 2

Thus, according to Confucian teachings, a government should regulate its people's conduct by means of Li, punishments and music; together they bring unity in the people's hearts and give effect to the principles of political order:

MUSIC RISES from the human heart. When the emotions are touched, they are expressed through sounds: when these sounds take definite forms, they produce music. Thus, a peaceful and prosperous country produces tranquil and joyous music and its government is orderly. When a country is in turmoil, its music shows dissatisfaction and anger, and its government is chaotic. When a country is in destruction, its music is full of sorrow and nostalgia, and people there are distressed. So we see music and government are inseparable from each other ... He who understands music is very close to understanding *Li*, and if a man has mastered both *Li* and music, then he is a man of virtue.

Yet, when we speak of a country which is cultivated in its music, we do not mean the music is complicated, nor its festival ceremonies very elaborate. When we hear the music of the ancestral temple of Zhou, it is played on red strings and a long board, accompanied by one singer and three men in the chorus; there is a certain restraint in its sounds. And when we see the ceremonies of the royal feast, with dark wine, raw fish and plain soup, there is a certain restraint in the flavours. Clearly the ancient kings did not institute rituals and music merely to satisfy our sensual desires, but to teach people real taste and help them to return to their true natures.

Book of Rites, chapter 17

MUSIC RISES from inside, while *Li* come from the outside. Therefore music is quiet and calm, whereas *Li* is formal. The really great music is also simple, and the truly great ritual is simple in form. When good music prevails, no one should feel dissatisfied; when proper rituals prevail, there is no hard work or struggle. When we say that the kow-tow to the king shows he rules the world, it shows the influence of *Li* and music. When a country manages to keep violence at a minimum, or rulers from other countries come for visits; when weapons are stored away and the five criminal laws are not in use, yet people have no worries and the emperor has no anger; then we may say good music prevails. When there is affection amongst parents and children, when there is respect amongst elders and juniors, and when the Emperor sets a good example, and when such extends to the rest of the people in the country, we may say the *Li* prevails.

Book of Rites, chapter 17

PEOPLE SHOULD be controlled through the *Li* and music instituted by the ancient kings. The sound of weeping and wailing and the dress for mourning are used to express sorrow at funerals. The bell, drum, shield and hatchet are used to celebrate peace and happiness. The wedding and ceremonies to celebrate boys' and girls' maturity are there to mark their sexuality. The contest between archers and feasts in villages are for the purpose of social intercourse. *Li* regulates people's feelings; music brings harmony to the country; the government establishes orders and punishments prevent crimes. When *Li*, music, punishments and governments are all in order, then the principle of political order is fully established.

Book of Rites, chapter 17

In a cosmos seen as correlative, while Li *was believed to sustain the order of the universe, music was said to bring harmony in the universe:*

MUSIC UNITES; ritual divides. Through union people show affection towards each other and through difference people learn to respect each other. When music proceeds, the society becomes unstructured, but when ritual proceeds, the society becomes rigid. Through the work of rituals and music, people's inner feelings and their external conduct become balanced. By establishing rituals, one has a sense of order and discipline. Through music and songs, people enter an atmosphere of peace ...

Truly great music brings harmony to the universe and great rites are manifest in the hierarchical structure within the universe. Harmony restores the order to the physical world ... *Li* and music are given to us in the physical world, and gods are for the spiritual world; together the world may live in love and piety. *Li* teaches piety for all occasions, music teaches love in various forms. When morality is manifested through rituals and music, we have what is called culture and it develops through the reigns of wise rulers ...

Harmony penetrates into all things, order places all things in their proper places. Music arises from Heaven, while *Li* is formed according to earthly patterns. If we upset the patterns of earth, the world will result in violence and disorder. To obtain the proper ritual and music, we need to understand the principle of Heaven and Earth ...

The wise men thus created heavenly music and earthly rituals. When *Li* and music are well established, Heaven and Earth will function in perfect order.

Book of Rites, chapter 17

HEAVEN IS high and the Earth is low, according to which there is the hierarchy between kings and ministers. As the high and low are arranged in different ranks, we attain the principle of social ranks. When we have the law of nature to govern action and reaction, we learn to differentiate the great and small. When all things are grouped and classified according to their natural ranks, we learn the principle of diversity in the animal world. Therefore according to the constellations of stars in the Heaven, the different shapes of mountains and rivers and all things on earth are formed. Hence we say the universe is based on *Li*, the principle of distinction.

When *Qi* separates, one part ascends to Heaven and the other descends to the Earth, according to the principles of Yin Yang. Together with Heaven and Earth, they interact with each other. Thus with thunder and lightning, there comes wind and rain, in which things are given life; with the rotation of seasons and the movements of sun and moon, they grow and prosper. Hence we say the universe is based on Music, the principle of harmony ...

While Music expresses the creative force of the natural world, *Li* reflects their creations. While Heaven represents the principle of eternal motion, the Earth represents the principle of stillness. With the principle of movement and rest, there comes life in Heaven and Earth. This is why the wise men speak about *Li* and music.

Book of Rites, chapter 17

However, it is important to note that Confucius is said to have regarded music only as

THE MEANS by which the achievements of government are exalted. It should not be the basis of a government. Therefore only when all the officials in the government are working together in perfect harmony, can there be truly harmonious music.

Kongcongzi, chapter 2

So what is the basis of a good government, or an ordered society? As Mencius taught, the root of empire is in the state; the root of the state is in the family; and the root of the family is in the individual. Therefore in the nine rules of governing a state, cultivating the individual's personal life was placed the first. In other words, when individuals are filled with humanity, an ideal society, which is ordered and harmonious, and free of crime and punishment, will be realised. This was one of the most important teachings of Confucius: self-realisation was the first step toward world peace:

WHEN THE personal life is cultivated, the family will be regulated; when the family is regulated, the state may be in order.

Great Learning, prefatory remarks

INDIVIDUALS

Thus it is taught in the Great Learning:

ROM THE Son of Heaven to the ordinary people, all must regard the cultivation of one's personal life as the basis of all things.

Great Learning, prefatory remarks

And by

ULTIVATING ONE'S own personal character, he [the ruler] may learn how to govern other people. Only by knowing how to govern the people, will one have the ability to govern the state and the world.

Doctrine of the Mean, chapter 19

RECTIFYING THE MIND AND HEART

While cultivation of one's personal life was perceived as an essential step in regulating one's family, building an ordered state and eventually in bringing world peace, rectifying one's mind or heart, Xin, was said to be the fundamental aspect of cultivating one's personal life.

IN ANCIENT times, he who wished to bring peace to the world first learned to govern the state. He who wished to govern the state first regulated his family. He who wished to regulate his family first cultivated his personal life. He who wished to cultivate his personal life first rectified his heart. He who wished to rectify his heart first learned to be sincere in his will. He who wished to be sincere in his will first needed to have knowledge; knowledge derives from all things in the universe.

Great Learning, prefatory remarks

According to Mencius, Xin, the human mind or heart, was the master of the human body:

KUNGTU ASKED, 'All are men, but some are great men and some are small men, how can this be?' Mencius replied, 'Those who follow their greater part are great men; those who follow their lesser part are small men.' Kungtu continued, 'All are men, but some follow the greater part of themselves and others follow the lesser part of themselves, how can this be?' Mencius replied, 'Eyes and ears do not think. They are impinged on by external things. When things come in contact with each other, ears and eyes merely transmit the action. It is for the mind to think and to receive what has been transmitted. When the mind fails to think, it fails to receive too. Eyes, ears and mind are endowed by Heaven. When a man sets his priority on the greater parts of his body, the lesser will not be able to obstruct him. It is this that makes him a great man.'

Mencius 6A:15

THE MAN who puts great emphasis on exercising his mind is the man who fully understands his true nature. In understanding his true nature, he understands the Way of Heaven. To serve Heaven is to guard one's mind and to nourish one's true nature ... Cultivate oneself and wait patiently. This way one may develop full potential.

Mencius 7A:1

An acolyte or guardian on a terrace in the Forest of Confucius, Qufu.

In other words, by preserving and exercising their minds, the ancient sages and worthies nourished their true nature. This true nature of man, as taught by Mencius, was endowed by Heaven. As Heaven was perceived to be perfect, human nature was believed to be innately good:

IT IS IN the utmost of a man's nature that he does good. What do I mean by good? If a man commits evil, he is guilty of denying his heavenly endowment. Each person has the feelings of piety, shame, respect and a sense of right and wrong. From the feeling of piety, there grows out humanity; from the feeling of shame there comes righteousness; from the feeling of respect, one learns to observe rites; from the sense of right and wrong, one attains wisdom. Humanity, righteousness, rites and wisdom may not be obtained externally, they are within our nature. We are not however always aware of them. That's why I say, 'Seek and you shall find it. Ignore it, and you shall lose it.' Men are different, some are more different than others. Such differences are caused by their failure to cling onto their heavenly endowment. It is written in the *Book of Songs*: 'Heaven gave birth to all men. It gave them life and the rules to follow. By holding onto them, men gain the virtue of perfection.'

Mencius 6A:6

MAN'S NATURE is innately good, just as it is natural for water to flow downwards. As no water can flow naturally upwards, no man is innately bad. When you strike water with force, it can splash above your head. By building dams, it can be forced uphill. But this is not of the nature of water, it is the result of using external force. A man can be made to do evil, but evil is not of his nature, it is the result of external influence.

Mencius 6A:2

However, Mencius also pointed out that as men were subject to external forces and influences, so their true nature may be obstructed. Under the influences of external forces, those who manage to hold on to the heavenly principles may 'gain the virtue of perfection', whereas those who surrender to outside influences may be in danger of losing their goodness and giving way to evil. It was suggested that the notion of different endowments by external, or physical, forces originated from Confucius's own teaching:

BY NATURE men are alike. By practice, men become far apart.

Analects 17:2

In Confucian cosmology, material forces meant the cosmic forces of Yin Yang and the Five Phases. They were regarded as the essential elements not only in the natural world, but also in society and human individuals. The five organs within the human body were thought to correspond to the Five Phases. While all human beings were born good by nature, their endowments of material force were believed to be different. Such differences were not only manifested through their different physical forms, but also through their different characters. It was believed that the sage was born as the result of Yin Yang being in balance and of the Five Phases rotating according to their proper order. In the opposite case, the good nature of man would be overshadowed by evil. The world thus consisted of different types of people, as was described by Chen Chun (1159–1223), an outstanding Song Neo-Confucian scholar:

I N MOST people, there are varied material forces. Some are exceptionally strong, because they have a great amount of Yang force. Others are very weak, because their Yin force is

Statue of Confucius at entry to the new Confucian Institute, Qufu.

stronger. Then there are others who are restless, violent, fierce and tough. This shows their Yang force is evil. Others are crafty and unreliable, for they possess the Yin force, which is evil. Some are accommodating. They easily revert to their good nature. Others are very stubborn and refuse to listen to any good words. They are not very different from birds and animals. All in all, it is the material forces that make them different.

CHEN CHUN, *Beixi ziyi 1:2*

However, this does not suggest that human individuals are passive subjects of material force. It was believed that while human beings might be subjected to external influences and might vary in kind, human nature was one and unchangeable, and 'innately good'. This concept was said to have originated from Confucius when he taught that:

FROM THE interaction of Yin Yang the Way is established. The Way is perfect and it is manifested in individual natures.

Book of Changes, 'Appended Remarks' Part I, chapter 5

It was fully developed by the great Neo-Confucian thinker Zhu Xi during the twelfth century in his theory of Li–Qi. The Li referred to in this theory is, confusingly enough, an entirely different word from Li meaning 'ritual', which we encountered earlier. According to Zhu Xi, Li was the principle or the ultimate nature, which existed in all things and transcended space and time and served as the ultimate source for any human and living existence. So all human beings shared the same Li, just as:

> THERE IS only one moon.
> Yet it shines on thousands of lakes and rivers at the same time.

ZHU XI, Theory of Li–Qi

Qi, also translated as the vital energy, was regarded as the counterpart of Li. It represented the material forces, which varied in forms. Through Qi, Heaven produced living things, including humans. As the endowment of Qi differed, all living things, even within the same kind, were therefore unique in their own ways. While Li was ultimately good, Qi, on the other hand, could be either good or bad. Therefore Zhu Xi also developed the concept of two kinds of nature: the original nature, Xing, and the developed nature, Qing – also translated as feelings. The original nature consisted of Li alone and it was good. The developed nature, however, was acquired through human interaction with the external environment. It consisted of different forms of Qi, and it could be either good or bad. Xin, the human mind, or heart, as the master of the body, was also thought to be the master of nature and feelings: nature was the principle of the mind and the feelings were the function of the mind. It was believed to have the capacity to command and unite man's nature and feelings. It was a vital aspect of human nature, as Confucius taught:

HOLD IT [mind] fast, and you preserve it. Let it go, and you lose it.

Analects 15:32

ONCE UPON a time, the forests of Mount Niu were beautiful. But since a big town was built nearby, men cut down its trees. How could it still be beautiful? However, after days the trees started to grow again; the rains and the dew also made it grow greenery. Then the cattle and the sheep came to pasture upon it. That is why the mountain looks so barren today. People think that there has never been anything growing

Roof tiles and finials, Forest of Confucius, Qufu.

there. But is this the true nature of the mountain? As for human beings, are their hearts naturally lacking in humanity and righteousness? A man loses his goodness like the mountain loses its trees. They are cut down day after day, so how can it retain its beauty? However with time he grows, and in the early hour of the day, by the air's tranquillity, like all other men, he senses what is right and what is wrong. But such senses seem to be remote as they are disturbed and destroyed by the work of the day. One disturbance comes after another; even the recuperation of the night may not restore the mountain to its original form. When this happens to a man, he is becoming more and more like a beast. Seeing him act like a beast, it is hard to imagine what was once his true nature. Therefore, things may only grow with proper care and nourishment; without care and nourishment they will only wither away. As Confucius said: 'Hold it fast, and you preserve it. Let it go, and you lose it.' Confucius was talking about the human mind/heart.

Mencius 6A:8

I AM FOND of fish, but I am also fond of bear's claws. If I must make a choice, I prefer bear's claws. I love life, but I also love righteousness. If I must make a choice, I will choose righteousness. I love life but there are things I love more than life; therefore I will able to avoid seeking life by any means. I hate death, but there are things I hate more than death. I therefore will not seek to escape my responsibilities. If a man is taught to desire life above all, how could he avoid by taking all means to save it? If a man is taught to hate death above all, why should he not to try to avoid taking risks at all costs? It is in the mind of all men to have desires above life and to hate more than death, yet what makes the worthy different is that they are able to preserve those ideals. When a traveller's life depended on a basket of rice or a bowl of soup, he would refuse taking them if they were offered to him in an insulting manner. If you simply throw food at a beggar, he would not take it. So what can a man gain if he accepts a large sum of money by losing righteousness and rites? Or should one take a position on the offer of grand palaces and the services of wives and concubines? Or should one help one's poor friends? Earlier on I said that even in the matter of life and death, one would not accept things under certain conditions, but now the matters are merely palaces, wives and concubines, or long time friends: they are too trivial to be considered. This is what I mean by losing one's true heart/mind.

Mencius 6A:10

HUMANITY IS the heart of man. Justice is the path for man. Alas for the man who has lost his path and can no longer trace it, and who has lost his heart and has no means to recover it. If one lost chickens and dogs, one could go out and look for them. But if one has lost one's heart, one has no means to recover it.

Mencius 6A:11

Therefore, to rectify one's heart was considered by Mencius to be most essential in one's self-cultivation:

IN NOURISHING one's mind, there is no better way than to cut down the number of desires. When a man has fewer desires, his mind is less likely to be affected by many things. When a man has many desires, his mind is more likely to be affected by a few things.

Mencius 7B:35

Imperial Vault of Heaven, Temple of Heaven, Beijing.

THE SAGE

WHEN HUNGRY, all food tastes sweet. When thirsty, all water tastes sweet. But this cannot determine the quality of food and drink. It is hunger and thirst that cause one's appetite. But hunger and thirst do not only affect one's mouth and stomach but also one's mind. Yet a man who is not affected by occasions as such is a man unlike all other men.

Mencius 7A:27

Here, a man who is unlike all other men refers to a man of superior quality. In the Confucian tradition, the sages are regarded as the greatest among all men:

ONLY WITH measure and compass will one make a perfect square and circle. Sages are the perfect examples for human relations.

Mencius 4A:2

THE ACTIONS of a sage set the way of the world. His movements set the order for the world. His words set the teaching for the world. People from afar respect him and those who are near never get tired of him.

Doctrine of the Mean, chapter 28

Yao and Shun, two legendary emperors in ancient China, were often regarded as perfect models for all humanity:

A PRINCE who wishes to act in princely way and a subject who wishes to behave as subject should take Yao and Shun as their models. In serving his prince, he who does not follow the model in which Shun served Yao is one who does not show reverence for his prince. He who fails to govern his people the way Yao did is one who deprives his people. As Confucius taught: 'There are only two ways for us, that of humanity or that of inhumanity.'

Mencius 4A:2

THE DIFFERENCES between men and beasts are minimal. Ordinary men are not aware of this. But a true gentleman guards his true nature carefully. Shun was such a person who did not only understand all living creatures but also knew the unique relationships between beings. Humanity and righteousness are the basis of human relationships and not the other way round.

Mencius 4B:19

Formal entry to dwelling, Forest of Confucius, Qufu.

IT IS BY carefully guarding humanity and rites in his thoughts that a true gentleman differs from other men. A man of humanity loves others. A man of rites knows how to respect. He who loves others is loved by others. He who respects others is also respected by others. A true gentleman always looks for the inner reason, and asks why things have happened, bearing in mind humanity and rites. If he has acted humanely and kept rites properly, yet bad things have kept on happening, he will re-examine himself again and find out where he has failed to do his best. But if he finds he has done all he could yet the bad things continue, he will say: 'Surely this person is incurable, I have certainly done with him. The way he behaves is barely different from a beast. Why should I be put out by a beast?' Therefore throughout his life a gentleman guards his thoughts carefully, not in a single day of worrying. These are things he thinks on carefully: 'Shun was a man like me. Yet Shun was a model for the world, a model throughout history, whereas I am merely a small man.' This is what he thinks carefully so that he might become like Shun. There is nothing that a true gentleman would be worrying over. He would not do things against humanity or things opposite to the rites.

Mencius 4B:28

CONSTANT VIRTUES

Clearly, humanity, Ren, was a core aspect of Confucian teachings. Confucius often used the term in the sense of human perfection. It was thought to be somehow an almost transcendental quality that was possessed by the semi-divine sages such as Yao and Shun. However, it was also thought that

THE STUPID can become intelligent and the weak can become strong.

Doctrine of the Mean, chapter 19

Mencius believed that 'all men can become Yao or Shun' (see also Er-Cheng Yishu, 18:17b) by cultivating humanity. The quality of humanity, however, as taught, first came from the feeling of love from, as well as towards, one's immediate family:

A TRUE gentleman may love all living things, yet he will not treat all things with humanity. He may treat all human beings with humanity, but he will not treat them all with affection. However, he who feels the love of family feels humanity towards all men. He who feels humanity towards all men loves all living things.

Mencius 7A:45

However, in Neo-Confucian teachings, as explained by Chen Chun, it is believed that the virtue of humanity also includes and commands the three other so-called constant virtues, namely righteousness, rites and wisdom:

WHAT DOES it mean when we say righteousness, rites and wisdom are all humanity? In a man of humanity, his mind is the Way of Heaven in operation, whereas the same Way of Heaven also operates in the three hundred rules of ritual and three thousands rules of conduct. So it is with righteousness. It operates by this Way of Heaven which puts all its thousands upon thousands of details in proper and right places. It is the same with wisdom. It operates by the same Way of Heaven which differentiates over tens of thousands of things and determines right and wrong amongst them.

CHEN CHUN, *Beixi ziyi 1:8*

Scholar's pavilion, birthplace of Mencius, Zou, Shandong Province.

According to Mencius, these four virtues were manifested through man's natural feelings:

EVERY MAN has feelings of pity, shame, respect and a sense of right and wrong. Humanity comes from the feeling of pity. Justice comes from the feeling of shame. The observance of rites is linked with one's feeling of respect. Wisdom comes from the sense of right and wrong. Humanity, justice, rites and wisdom cannot be apart; they are within our very nature.

Mencius 6A:6

They should therefore be reflected through human relationships:

BETWEEN FATHER and son there should be humanity. Between the ruler and his subjects, there should be righteousness. Between man and woman, they should attain their different functions by observing the rites. Between old and young, they should attain the right order through wisdom. Between friends, there should be faithfulness.

Mencius 3A:4

Here Mencius taught the fifth constant virtue, faithfulness, Xin, as the basis of relationships between friends. However, in Confucian teachings, this word Xin is often used together with the word Zhong – commonly translated as loyalty – applied to more than just relationships between friends to include also all human relationships. Zhong-Xin in the Confucian tradition was thought not to occur due to human nature, but through human effort. Its meanings were rather complex. Apart from faithfulness and loyalty, it could also mean honesty, truthfulness, sincerity and trustworthiness.

I F A MAN is unreliable, he will lose respect from those below him as well as the foundation on which he can progress. A gentleman must first learn to be faithful to his superiors, to keep his promises and not to make friends with those who are not like him. If he has made a mistake, he must not be afraid of admitting it and correcting it.

Analects 1:8

M INISTERS MUST serve their ruler in complete devotion.

Analects 3:19

I EXAMINE myself daily on these three things: have I always been loyal to their interests when acting on behalf of others? Have I always been true to my own word in dealing with friends? Have I forgotten what was handed down to me from the times before?

Analects 1:4

In the Doctrine of the Mean, Xin *was taken to mean trustworthiness, which was thought to be derived from sincerity,* Cheng.

FOR THOSE who are in the position below, it is impossible to govern people if one does not have trust, *Xin*, from one's superior. There is only one way of gaining trust from the superior: if one does not have the trust from one's friends, one may not be trusted by one's superior. There is only one way of gaining trust from one's friends: if one is not filial towards one's parents, one cannot gain trust from one's friends. There is only one way of being filial: if one is not sincere, one is not being filial towards one's parents. There is only one way of being sincere: if one does not know what is good, one cannot be sincere.

Doctrine of the Mean, chapter 19

Papier-mâché figures of sacrificial animals at a ceremony loosely based on Confucian ritual descriptions. Performers wear Manchu dress. Confucian Temple, Qufu.

It was taught that

TO BE sincere in one's will means not to deceive oneself.

Great Learning, chapter 4

Apart from the above meanings, some later tradition suggests that Xin could also mean to have faith, or to believe, as the final translation from Japanese, below, makes clear.

In the Doctrine of the Mean, sincerity, Cheng, was regarded as the Way of Heaven, a virtue of the sages, whereas to be sincere, or to be truthful, was said to be a moral principle for all men. One's very nature could only be fulfilled through sincerity and truthfulness. A society, and different levels of human relationships, could only be functional on the basis of sincerity and truthfulness:

SINCERITY, CHENG, is the Way of Heaven. To be sincere is the principle for all men. A man of sincerity attains harmony without much effort and gains knowledge easily without thinking hard day and night. The one who can easily attain harmony and knows the Way of nature is a sage. A sincere man is one who knows what is good and holds to it steadfastly.

Doctrine of the Mean, chapter 19

ONLY WHEN there is sincerity and truthfulness in the world will its true nature be manifested. When the world attains its true nature, men can then fulfil their human nature. When human nature is fulfilled, all living things may sustain their own very nature. When all things retain their very nature, we may be able to appreciate all creation in Heaven and on the Earth. Only in praise of all creation, may we be able to live in harmony with Heaven and Earth.

Doctrine of the Mean, chapter 21

THE PRINCIPLE of sincerity and truthfulness can foretell the future. If a country or family is about to prosper, there must be lucky signs. If a country and family is about to decline, there must be unlucky signs. We can foretell the coming of disasters and good luck in forms of divination and through the human body. We know beforehand whether the good is coming or whether the bad is coming. When the principle of sincerity and truthfulness is fulfilled, one may obtain the spirit of the divine.

Doctrine of the Mean, chapter 23

THUS, *CHENG* is the Way of Heaven, the foundation and the principle of all things. *Cheng* is the beginning and the end of all things. Without *Cheng*, there is nothing. That is why the sages always put *Cheng* first. The principle of *Cheng* should not only be fulfilled within oneself, it should also be fulfilled in all things. In a person *Cheng* manifests itself through humanity; in things *Cheng* manifests itself through wisdom. Although they seem to be different from the outside, they are the two virtues of the one true nature. By combining both, one will know the right time and the right thing.

Doctrine of the Mean, chapter 23

Confucian statuary, birthplace of Mencius.

When the true nature of a man was fulfilled, he could be called a sage, a perfect individual according to the Confucian tradition. Such a man should be:

ABLE, INTELLIGENT, has heard and seen all things, and understands all things. He also possesses all the qualities for governing the world: humanity, righteousness, rites and wisdom. He is therefore generous and gentle, which enables him to exercise patience. He is also strong and determined, which enables him to carry out his duty. He has both dignity and integrity, and therefore is highly revered and respected. He is both knowledgeable and careful, and therefore has a good sense of judgement.

Doctrine of the Mean, chapter 30

THE TRUE GENTLEMAN

While sagehood was encouraged to be the ultimate aim for all mankind, a sage was also thought to be equal to Heaven. On a more human level, as already mentioned, Confucian teachings frequently speak of the way of true gentlemen. According to Confucius, a true gentleman

CULTIVATES IN himself the quality so that he is diligent in his work … he cultivates in himself the ability to unload other people's burdens.

Analects 14:45

A TRUE GENTLEMAN may lack for goodness but there is never a good man who is not a true gentleman.

Analects 14:7

IN FOLLOWING the Way, there are three things that a gentleman holds the highest: he shows no signs of violence or arrogance in all he does; all his expressions must be sincere; he must not speak any dirty or improper words.

Analects 8:4

A TRUE GENTLEMAN has no griefs or fears.

Analects 12:4

A TRUE GENTLEMAN always points out the goodness in others but does not speak loudly of their faults.

Analects 12:16

G ENTLEMEN NEVER compete with each other. In the case of archery, they bow and make way for each other to start; then drink to each other when they finish. So even in competition, they remain gentlemen.

Analects 3:7

A TRUE GENTLEMAN is easy to serve, but hard to please. He refuses to be pleased by those who do not follow the Way, but he does not have a high expectation from those who serve him.

Analects 13:25

An acolyte or guardian on a terrace in the Forest of Confucius, Qufu.

A TRUE GENTLEMAN is dignified yet without pride.

Analects 13:26

A TRUE GENTLEMAN is proud but not quarrelsome. He is friendly with individuals but never associates himself with parties.

Analects 15:21

A TRUE GENTLEMAN is ashamed if he preaches without deeds.

Analects 14:29

T HERE ARE three qualities that a true gentleman has, yet I have not succeeded in any of them. He who is good is never unhappy, he who is wise never confuses people and he who is brave is never afraid.

Analects 14:30

A TRUE GENTLEMAN does not grieve if people do not recognise his merits, yet he grieves at his own want of abilities.

Analects 14:32

A TRUE GENTLEMAN establishes righteousness as the basis for all his conduct and uses rites to guide his actions. He is modest in what he does yet never fails to complete his task.

Analects 15:17

A TRUE GENTLEMAN makes demands upon himself but not on others.

Analects 15:20

A TRUE GENTLEMAN does not accept a man because of what he says, or reject sayings because of the speaker.

Analects 15:22

WHEN A gentleman makes a plan, he follows the Way, he does not consider how to make a living, even if there might be a shortage of food, and even if learning might be costly. But a true gentleman is concerned with the progress of the Way, he is not anxious about poverty.

Analects 15:31

IN HIS own home village, he is simple and attentive, and slow to speak. Yet at the ancestral temple and at court, he speaks correctly with authority. When he talks to junior ministers he is friendly and affable. When he talks to senior ministers he is humble and well mannered. When he talks to the ruler he is cautious but not nervous …

A true gentleman will not wear blue and purple for outdoors nor will he wear pink or red for indoors. In summer he wears a fine quality unlined gown, but when he goes out he puts on an outer garment. With a black lambskin coat he matches a black robe; with a fawn coat he matches a plain robe. With a fur coat, he matches a yellow robe. He always wears a nightgown that covers up all his body, yet the right is shorter than the left (so he can move freely). What he wears for bed is however half the length of his body. He wears thick fur at home. Except when he is in mourning, he wears all the ornaments that show his class …

He must eat a variety of foods at different places. The rice he eats should be the highest quality of all and the minced meat can never be fine enough for him. He must not eat rice that is off, or fish that is not fresh, or meat that is tainted. He must not eat anything that has changed colour or smells bad. He must not eat anything that is overcooked or undercooked. He should not eat anything that is out of season. He must not eat anything that

Statue of Confucius at entry to the new Confucian Institute, Qufu.

is not properly prepared or seasoned. He should not eat more meat than rice so that his breath smells. There is no limit for the drinks, yet he must not be drunk. He must not take any drinks or eat any cured meat from the market; but he may eat food that is prepared with ginger. However, he must not overeat.

Analects 10:6, 8

A TRUE GENTLEMAN puts righteousness first ... he hates those who hate others. He hates those in low positions who envy those above. He hates those who are courageous but neglect rituals. He hates those who are restless and adventurous, but have a violent temper.

Analects 17:23–4

THERE ARE three things that a true gentleman guards against. In his youth when he is passionate, he must guard against lust. When he has reached his prime, his blood is full and he is strong, so he must guard against being quarrelsome. When he is old and his body begins to slow down, he must guard against being greedy.

Analects 17:7

THERE ARE three things a true gentleman holds in awe: the mandate of Heaven, men of greatness and the sayings of sages.

Analects 16:8

THERE ARE nine things a true gentleman cares about: seeing clearly; hearing distinctly; looking kindly; conducting himself respectfully; loyalty to his own words; and diligence in his own work. When in doubt he inquires carefully; when in anger, he is concerned for the consequences; when he sees a chance, he considers it carefully in order to make the right judgement.

Analects 16:10

A TRUE GENTLEMAN never eats till he is sitting down. He does not demand the comfort of home and is diligent in his work. He is careful in his speech. He associates himself with those who possess the Way in order to correct his own faults. He is the one who is yearning for learning.

A true gentleman widens his knowledge by learning, and he uses the knowledge to refrain from making mistakes.

Analects 6:25

Clearly, according to Confucian teachings, education was an essential aspect of self-cultivation.

EDUCATION

In the Confucian tradition, education was given very high, if not the highest, priority. It was believed that individuals could only attain the highest human virtue, humanity, Ren, *through education. The education of an individual is a path to a peaceful and ordered society:*

HUMAN NATURE is given by Heaven. To fulfil it is the *Dao*, the Way of Heaven. The cultivation of the *Dao* is called education.

Doctrine of the Mean, prefatory remarks

TO BE fond of learning brings one close to knowledge. To make a real effort in one's action brings one close to humanity. To know shame brings one close to courage. He who knows these three things knows the way of cultivating himself. By knowing the way of self-cultivation, one knows how to govern people. By knowing how to govern people, one knows how to rule the world and the country.

Doctrine of the Mean, chapter 19

HE WHO studies widely and purposefully, he who questions earnestly, and he who thinks carefully on what he has heard is the one to achieve goodness.

Analects 19:6

TO DESIRE goodness without love of learning may lead to foolishness. To desire wisdom without love of learning may lead to dissipation of mind. To be faithful in keeping promises but without love of learning may bring harm. To desire righteousness without love of learning may lead to harshness. To desire courage without love of learning may lead to troubles. To be strict without love of learning may result in unreasonable conduct.

Analects 17:8

BY INVESTIGATING things one obtains knowledge. With extension of knowledge, one learns to be sincere in one's will. When one is sincere one can then rectify one's heart. By rectifying one's heart, one may cultivate one's personal life. Through cultivation of one's personal life, one may regulate the family. When the family is regulated, one may govern the State. By governing the State, there may be peace in the world.

Great Learning, prefatory remarks

B Y DESIRING righteousness and seeking after goodness one may gain a small reputation but will not be able to influence the masses. To be close to the wise and the able, and to welcome those who come from afar might help a person to influence others, but he cannot cultivate others. Therefore a true gentleman can only cultivate others and establish a good social order by means of education. This is like a piece of jade; without chiselling, it cannot become a work of art; a man without education cannot understand moral principles. Thus the kings of ancient times considered education to be foremost in their efforts to establish the social order of their countries. This is what is meant in the *Book of History* when it says 'always bear in mind education'. Just as one cannot know the taste of food without eating it, without education one cannot know the greatness of an extensive body of knowledge, no matter how great it might be.

Book of Rites, chapter 16

Roof tiles and finials, Forest of Confucius, Qufu.

It is therefore not surprising that Confucius himself devoted his whole life to education, either as a student or as a teacher:

A T THE age of fifteen I set my heart upon learning. At the age of thirty, I had my feet firmly on the ground. At the age of forty, I was no longer confused. At the age of fifty, I knew the ways of Heaven. At the age of sixty, my ears became used to them [the ways of Heaven]. At the age of seventy, I could follow what my heart desired without fear of transgression.

Analects 2:4

G IVE ME a few more years so that I may complete my fifty years of study, and then I will surely avoid making any major errors.

Analects 7:16

I AM NOT one who was born with knowledge. I am one who simply loves the ways of the ancients and makes a great effort to learn them.

Analects 7:19

SAGE OR a true gentleman, I am far from being either and I do not dare to make any claim. But I never become bored of studying and never get tired of teaching. These are the merits I am not ashamed to claim.

Analects 7:33

I HAVE PASSED on what was taught to me without adding anything of my own. I have been faithful and devoted to the past ... I have listened silently and accumulated knowledge; when I study, I do not get bored; when teaching others I do not become weary. These are the merits I can claim confidently.

Analects 7:1–2

To LEARN and to repeat from time to time what one has learned, is that not a pleasure after all?

Analects 1:1

THE TEACHER

In the early Confucian tradition, it was often taught that through education, one could achieve the goal of becoming a morally superior person, a true gentleman:

IT IS impossible to be a gentleman without self-cultivation. Yet it is impossible to imagine a cultivated person who does not show affection to his relatives. It is however impossible to show affection without knowing the person. Yet it is difficult to understand people without knowing the Way of Heaven …

Some people are born with knowledge. Some people acquire knowledge through learning. Some people gain knowledge through hardship in life. But the knowledge they obtain is the same. Some might find it is easy to put it into practice; some might find it is beneficial to practise it, whereas others might find it is difficult to carry it out in action. But when they finally succeeded, the result is the same.

Doctrine of the Mean, chapter 19

It was taught that a true gentleman will influence the world through his teaching:

Imperial Vault of Heaven, Temple of Heaven, Beijing.

FOR SOME, as with dried earth in a season of drought,
May be transformed by his teaching;
Some may fulfil their virtue by his teaching;
Some may expand their talents by his teaching;
Some may find answers in his teaching;
And others may indirectly benefit from it.
It is for these five reasons that he offers instruction.

Mencius 7A:40

*Teachers therefore were often held in high regard in the
Confucian tradition:*

DRUM IS not one of the five sounds of music, yet the five
sounds cannot be in harmony without the drum. Water is
not one of the five colours, yet the five colours cannot
shine without water. Learning is not one of the five senses, yet
the five senses cannot come about without learning. A teacher
is not one of the five clans [family relations], yet the five clans
cannot love each other without a teacher.

Book of Rites, chapter 16

IN EDUCATION, the most difficult thing is to respect teachers. Only when a teacher is respected will people then respect his teaching. When people respect his teaching, they then respect learning and scholarship. Therefore there are two kinds of people a king pays high regard to: his teacher, and the mediator of the spirits. Traditionally, at school a teacher does not need to stand facing north even when he is receiving an edict from the king. This shows great respect for teachers.

Book of Rites, chapter 16

However, a good teacher, it was believed, should never stop learning:

THROUGH EDUCATION one becomes dissatisfied with one's knowledge, but through teaching others one becomes uncomfortable with the inadequacy of one's knowledge. When dissatisfied, one recognises the trouble within oneself. When uncomfortable, one becomes eager to improve oneself. As it is said: 'Teaching and learning stimulate one another.' This is what was meant in the *Book of Changes*: 'Teaching is the half of learning.'

Book of Rites, chapter 16

Other than constant learning, a teacher, it was said, should possess the following qualities:

B Y KNOWING how to succeed in education and the cause of its failure, a true gentleman is then qualified to be a teacher. Thus, in his teaching, a true gentleman guides his students but does not force them. He encourages them to advance and does not suppress them. He opens a path for them but does not carry them there. Guidance without force makes the learning pleasant. Encouragement without suppressing eases up the learning. Opening the way without carrying them there makes students think. This is what we call a good teacher.

Book of Rites, chapter 16

T HERE ARE four common mistakes in education a teacher must be aware of. Some students study too much and too many subjects whereas others study too little and too few subjects. Some students find study too easy whereas others give up studying too easily. This is because each individual differs in their mental capacity, and by knowing this a teacher can avoid making these mistakes. A teacher should be the person to bring out the goodness and to remedy the weaknesses of his students.

Book of Rites, chapter 16

A GOOD SINGER leads others to follow his tune, a good teacher causes others to follow his ideal. His words should be short yet sharp, casual yet deep. He is also illustrative, so that people can understand him easily. In this way he can be seen as a good example for men to follow.

A true gentleman knows what are the difficult and easy things, as well as the good and the deplorable things in learning. He is also very illustrative. Being illustrative he shows he has the quality to be a teacher. With the quality of being a teacher, he then has the quality of being an elder. With the quality of being an elder, he can then know how to govern others. Thus, the art of being a teacher is the art of learning to be a ruler. It is therefore important to select one's teacher carefully. This is what was meant in the Book of Changes: 'The Three Kings and Four Dynasties emphasised the foremost in selecting teachers.'

Book of Rites, chapter 16

THERE ARE many ways of teaching. By the very thing I do not think worth teaching, I teach a man something.

Mencius 6B:16

THOSE WHO only possess knowledge by memorising so that they may be able to answer questions are not fit to be teachers. A good teacher should listen to the conversation of students. When he sees a student has failed after trying his best, the teacher should try to explain to him [a bit more], and if the student fails to understand after the explanation, then he should not pursue the matter.

Book of Rites, chapter 16

A TEACHER MUST teach with complete detachment. When it [teaching] is not working, he may show his anger. But if a father shows anger, he causes pain to his son. My teacher taught me with complete detachment and he never forsook this principle. But it is painful for both father and son to become detached from each other. It is unfortunate when father and son cause pain to each other. Therefore in ancient times, fathers only taught the sons of others.

Mencius 4A:19

To those who are not eager to learn I do not explain anything, and to those who are not bursting to speak I do not reveal anything. If I raise one angle and they do not come back with the other three angles, I will not repeat myself.

Analects 7:8

He who by studying the knowledge of the past gains new knowledge is fit to be a teacher.

Analects 2:11

In the Neo-Confucian tradition education was often seen as being preferable to punishment:

In ancient times, punishment was rarely used, but today it is highly prevalent. The reason for this is that in ancient times people were first taught rites, punishment only came secondarily. Today, rites are not taught, people are restricted by means of punishment. That is why punishments are prevalent today.

Kongcongzi 4:1

Formal entry to dwelling, Forest of Confucius, Qufu.

TIAN-LI, THE PRINCIPLE OF HEAVEN

By expanding the teachings in the Great Learning, Neo-Confucianists such as Zhu Xi and Chen Chun fostered the concept that the ultimate purpose of education is to retain the Principle of Heaven, Tian-Li:

THE WAY of Heaven is so vast, where does one begin? ... The extension of knowledge means to understand in one's heart all the principles of the universe without any doubt. Being earnest means to work hard without any negligence. To practise it earnestly means to recover all the goodness within oneself and make sure there is none missing. Without the extension of knowledge, it is difficult to know what is true and what is false, so how can one know which way to practise? It is therefore likely that one will mistake human desires for the Principle of Heaven without actually realising it. However without practising earnestly, although [one might know] the essential principle metaphysically, in reality it will be nothing but empty words. So how can great virtue and perfect goodness manifest through oneself? That is why the *Great Learning* teaches that to manifest bright virtue one must begin with investigating things and expanding knowledge, then follow on with sincerity in one's will, rectification of one's heart and self-cultivation. According to the *Doctrine of the Mean*, in order to choose what is good and to hold on to it, one must follow the order of expanding one's knowledge, keeping on asking questions, thinking carefully, making clear one's judgement and practising earnestly.

CHEN CHUN, Beixi ziyi, 'Lectures at Yanling' 3

JUST AS all apprentices must stay in their [different] workshops to perfect their skills, through study a true gentleman improves according to the Way.

Analects 19:7

One of Confucius's favourite disciples, Yan Hui, was often used as an example in carrying out the programme of expanding knowledge and practice earnestly:

THERE WAS Yan Hui – he truly loved learning. He had never shown anger to the innocent or let others suffer because of his faults. But Heaven endowed him with such a short life. He has now died, and there is no one that can compare with him in his fondness for learning.

Analects 6:2

WHEN YAN Hui praised the Master [Confucius] for being patient, skilful and inspiring in the way he taught, he only mentioned that 'he expanded me [my knowledge] with literature and restrained me with rites' and nothing else. However, these two should not be divided into the order of first and second. It is like walking: one sees with the eyes and walks with the feet. Both movements correspond to each other and each advances and stimulates the other. Therefore, if one has clear knowledge, in practice one can go further; whereas if one practises earnestly, one's knowledge will become more sophisticated.

In expanding knowledge and earnest practice, the most fundamental thing is reverence. By reverence it basically means when we concentrate on one thing and do not depart from it. Therefore one's heart always remains cautious and the mind is on the alert. This is the way to keep the mind alive, and exhibits the success of sagely knowledge in penetrating into one's activity and tranquillity from the beginning to the end. With reverence, one's inner self is cultivated and one knows the fundamentals clearly. If, by basing oneself on this, one can expand one's knowledge, one's mind will then go hand in hand with principle; there will be no worries of being bored or being stupid. If, by basing oneself on this, one practises earnestly,

Scholar's pavilion, birthplace of Mencius, Zou, Shandong Province.

one's body and affairs will be at peace with each other; there will be no conflict of one with the other ...

One must be like Yanzi, who was able yet not ashamed of asking the less able; who knew much yet was not ashamed of asking those who knew less; who had much yet acted as if he had nothing; who was full [of knowledge] yet was modest. Only then was he able to be modest to his heart. Once one is ambitious without self-pity, yet modest in heart and not full of oneself, only then may one follow the hard-working programme set out by the sages. Renewing oneself and benefiting from it day after day, one can then ascend to the hall [of examination] and enter [the teacher's] room, and act as one desires without any obstacles. Scholars should bear this deep [in their hearts] and use this as a guard to warn [themselves].

CHEN CHUN, *Beixi ziyi*, '*Lectures at Yanling*' 3

GREAT LEARNING AND SMALL LEARNING

Zhu Xi further divided education into two kinds of learning: the 'great learning' and the 'small learning'. It was taught that the 'great learning' consisted of the principles of education, whereas the 'small learning' was said to consist of daily work at home, polite conversation and manners, the study and practice of rituals, music, archery, calligraphy and so on. It was said that it should begin with children. The model of both learnings should be based on the system of ancient times:

THE FOLLOWING was the ancient education system. In a village, amongst every twenty-five families, there was a primary school. In a town, amongst every five hundred families, there was a secondary school. In a country, amongst every two thousand and five hundred families there was an academy, and there was a university in the capital of every state.

Every year new students were admitted. There was an examination in between the years. Towards the end of the first year, a great effort was made to teach students the correct way to punctuate sentences and to find out their likes and dislikes. Towards the end of the third year, a great effort was made in knowing their habits of study and [to teach them] to live in groups. Towards the end of the fifth year, a great effort was made in students' reading efficiency and [to encourage] them to follow their teachers closely. Towards the end of the seventh year, the students would then have developed the ability to think for themselves and to choose friends for themselves. This was the so-called 'small achievement'. Towards the end of the ninth year, the students should have become familiar with various subjects and acquired a general knowledge about life, and established a solid foundation for their personality which could no longer be altered. This was the so-called 'great achievement'.

Book of Rites, chapter 16

ONLY WITH an education system as such is it then possible to cultivate people and to improve the moral standards of the country. This way all people of the country will be happy and people from afar will come to the country. This is the principle of Great Learning.

In the university, students should study how to use ceremonial robes and how to offer sacrifice with vegetables. This way they will learn the principle of respect and piety. They should sing the first three songs of the third section of the Book of Songs so that they learn the basics of official life. When entering the university, the first thing is to strike a drum before students open their books. This is to teach them about discipline. A stick is used to teach them proper behaviour. No inspector is sent to the university except on the grand occasion of offering sacrifice to the royal ancestors. This way, students may be able to develop on their own. A teacher should observe more instead of constantly lecturing, so that students may be able to think about things for themselves. Junior students should listen more instead of asking questions, so that they may know where they stand. These seven are the main methods in education.

Book of Rites, chapter 16

Papier-mâché figures of sacrificial animals at a ceremony loosely based on Confucian ritual descriptions. Performers wear Manchu dress. Confucian Temple, Qufu.

THE BENEFITS OF EDUCATION

Education, it was believed, was beneficial for individuals and for society:

I N THE university education system, there are regular classes and free study periods amongst students in their own rooms. Without practice with one's fingers, one cannot learn to play any string instrument smoothly. Without wide observation of all things, one cannot learn the poetry in [the Book of Songs] easily. Without the knowledge of how to use different ceremonial robes, one cannot master rituals. Without learning various [physical] arts, one will not know the joy of schooling. Therefore, when [one is] educating a gentleman, he should be given the time to digest and to cultivate things, as well as the time to rest and to play. In this way students will feel at home in the university, and will establish a close relationship with their teachers; they will know the joy of friendship and will gain the ability to form their own ideas. Then when they leave their teachers, they will not give up studying.

Book of Rites, chapter 16

MOST WELL-TO-DO families teach their younger members to read in the firm hope that they will pass their examinations for the civil service or go on to undertake further study into the subtleties of the words and deeds of the great and good. But fate decrees that some succeed and others do not; by nature some are bright, others less so – you cannot expect of the young that they will always reach their goal. Yet it is quite out of the question that they should be made to stop studying because they are not achieving.

For when young people read books they partake of what ancient Daoist philosophers called 'the usefulness of the useless'. Reading history provides a fund of stories, literature a store of fine phrases. Even books on astrology and the occult and popular fiction contain some diverting passages. Since there are volumes upon volumes of books – more than can be read in months or even years – young people immersed in them all day are bound to derive some benefit from them and will not have time for other pursuits. They are also sure to make friendships with those who have been in the business of scholarship for a while, mixing with them and engaging them in discussion. What chance then of their spending their days well provided for but making no use of their minds, and so getting mixed up in wrongdoing with common hooligans?

YUAN CAI, *Yuanshi shifan, 1:14*

BOOKS

Book reading and tradition were synonymous in Confucian education, and books were regarded as vehicles of the Way. However, these were not just ordinary books but the Confucian Classics. Zhu Xi was one of the foremost (if not the only) promoters of the Confucian Classics. He canonised the Confucian Classics in what has been known as the Four Books *– the* Great Learning, *the* Analects, *the* Mencius *and the* Doctrine of the Mean *– which he believed to be the kernel of the Confucian teachings. And it was through the effort of Zhu Xi and others that the* Four Books *became widely studied by the common people. From the Yuan Dynasty (1271–1368), they became the primary texts for the civil service examinations throughout imperial China. In Neo-Confucian practice there were certain rules and orders for studying the* Four Books, *of which the* Great Learning *was given the priority:*

IF ONE does not study the *Great Learning* first, then one cannot grasp the structure of learning, and then one cannot understand fully the *Analects* and the *Book of Mencius*. If one does not read the *Great Learning* together with the *Analects* and the *Book of Mencius*, then one cannot understand fully all the connections between them, and thus one will not

be able to grasp the essence of the *Doctrine of the Mean* ...
Thus any student must study the *Four Books* earnestly, and to
study the *Four Books* one must begin with the *Great Learning*.

Zhu Xi, Commentary on the Great Learning

BOOKS ARE vehicles of the Way; therefore no one should
avoid reading them. However, the teachings and the
sayings of the sages and the great are not all the same,
they were endowed with an order of procession and urgency;
each should not be skipped. Master Cheng [Cheng Yi] taught:
'The *Great Learning* is a legacy of Confucius, it is the gateway
through which any beginner enters into virtue. We now know
the order in which the ancients carried out their study; it
primarily relied on what was preserved in this book, whereas
the *Analects* and the *Book of Mencius* came after [it]. When
studying, scholars must follow this [order]; this is the way to
avoid making any mistakes.'

Chen Chun, Beixi ziyi, 'Lectures at Yanling' 4

THE *GREAT LEARNING* was the basic rule of adult education for the ancients. Its essential points are these three: the so-called 'manifestation of the clear [good] virtue', 'renewal in people' and 'abiding in the ultimate goodness'. Amongst these three, they were further divided into eight steps: from investigation of things, expansion of knowledge, sincerity of the will, rectification of the heart and self-cultivation to regulating the family, governing the state and bringing peace to the world. Its contents are vast and broad but do not lose the essential points. The programme is very detailed yet without any confusion. It is truly the main outline of the Classics and scholars must explain it clearly first.

CHEN CHUN, *Beixi ziyi*, *'Lectures at Yanling'* 4

THERE ARE the twenty chapters of the *Analects*. It is the collection of the most important sayings and deeds of the Master. By studying it, one will gain solid knowledge of how to retain and nurture human nature.

CHEN CHUN, *Beixi ziyi*, *'Lectures at Yanling'* 4

THE SEVEN Books of *Mencius* … are all philosophical discussions on the subject of the kingly way, humanity and righteousness. By studying them one will attain the ultimate experience and be enriched.

CHEN CHUN, Beixi ziyi, 'Lectures at Yanling' 4

THE ONE book of the *Doctrine of the Mean* … is the law of the mind passed on by the Confucian school. Master Cheng thought it was so interesting that one could go back to study it over and over again. A skilful reader contemplates and always benefits from it; he can apply it all his life with no limit. However, as its words generally are more to do with higher meanings and less concerned with low level study, it is not something for any beginning students to discuss. They must have understood thoroughly the *Great Learning*, the *Analects*, and the *Mencius* before they come to [study] this [the *Doctrine of the Mean*]. They will then begin to know it as solid knowledge, not as something that is unclear.

CHEN CHUN, Beixi ziyi, 'Lectures at Yanling' 4

I F ONE does not read the *Great Learning* first, then one cannot grasp the essence of and discuss the details in the *Analects* and the *Mencius*. Without consulting the *Analects* and the *Mencius*, there is no way to discover the hidden treasures and to enjoy the ultimate goal of the *Doctrine of the Mean*. But without the ultimate goal that is in the *Doctrine of the Mean*, how can one establish the foundation for the world and bring out the best in human nature? This is why those who are seeking after the way cannot but be devoted in reading the *Four Books*.

The rule of reading the *Four Books* is not to expect too much, nor to try to be too clever, nor to seek out unimportant things, nor to twist their original meanings. Also one must remain calm and contemplate their meaning and objectives, and at the same time find what are the practical applications to oneself. If one can understand the *Four Books* thoroughly and apply them easily, the moral principle will be clear and shining and one will be subtle and cool, and thus able to make a right judgement. When one uses this [rule] as the starting point to read all the Classics, to read all the books in the world and to discuss world affairs, all [obstacles] will disappear like ice melting away. Width and length will be clearly defined, there will not be the slightest error. Alas, only when one has achieved this can one then go on to discuss the way of the sage and kingly way, and to open up resources successfully and accomplish great things.

CHEN CHUN, *Beixi ziyi, 'Lectures at Yanling' 4*

Although in practical terms in imperial China many of those who pursued learning had the desire of passing civil service examinations, so that they could obtain a good position in government, the ultimate goal of education, which was to retain the Principle of Heaven or to recover the goodness within human nature, was held in higher regard and was believed to be beneficial and not a hindrance to those who were preparing for the examinations.

SOME MAY also ask how to compare those who study for civil service examinations to the learning of the sages. The answer is that it is the same yet not exactly the same. They all study the same Classics and the same historical books, yet those who study for civil service examinations read only what is skin deep in order to write for the examinations. They do not get the taste of the inner meanings of [these works].

[Those who] only look out for what it seems to be and its general meanings, may be good at talking about them, but they cannot gain the knowledge of right or wrong. All day and night they scan information and read widely, and memorise, yet it is like arranging a lavish wedding, an unproductive exercise. [In the end] one cannot grasp any concrete moral principle …

Certain elements within civil service examinations might spoil the objective of sages and the wise, yet the learning of sages and the wise has never been a hindrance to literary writings for civil service examinations. When moral principles are clearly understood, writings and discussions reflect a brilliance of spirit. The one who is diligent in practising moral principles and taking them into his heart will manifest [them] through his discussion of current affairs and his suggestions for shaping up government policies. Every outer expression will be an overflowing of his inner self. So he will naturally respond to human feelings and adjust to the principle of things; he is amiable with words of humanity, righteousness and virtue, and all his words are applicable in every situation. If someone spots him with sharp eyes, he will become useful to the country, and that is far more important than being first [in the examination].

CHEN CHUN, *Beixi ziyi*

Confucian statuary, birthplace of Mencius.

[A CULTURED PERSON], was he who was diligent and fond of learning, and he was not ashamed to ask questions of those beneath him.

Analects 5:14

AFTER IN-DEPTH study and a long period of discussion one may again describe a matter with no mistake.

Mencius 4B:15

HE WHO learns without thinking is lost; he who thinks without studying is in danger.

Analects 2:15

TODAY MANY teachers repeat things over and over again; they annoy students with endless and repetitive questions. They do not attempt to find out the interests of their students; therefore the students only pretend to like study and do not try their best. It is the wrong thing that the teachers have offered to their students in the first place, and what they have been expecting from their students is also wrong. Therefore, the students hide away [the books] they love to read and dislike their teachers. They are unhappy with the difficulties in their studies and cannot see the benefit of [education]. Although they still go through the process of study, they do not pursue any further [studies] after graduation. This is why the present education system has failed.

Book of Rites, chapter 16

WITH GOOD students, a teacher only puts in a little effort yet the result is greater, and he gains respect from the students. With poor students, a teacher must work hard but with little result, and he is hated by the students. A man who is good at asking questions acts as if chopping wood; he starts with the easier end and leaves the knots to the last. By spending time together, teachers and students may reach a common understanding with a sense of pleasure. The poor ones achieve the opposite result. To know who is to answer questions is like to know how to strike bells. When one strikes with the big hammer, the big bell rings. It is also important [to know] that it will take time for its sounds to disappear. Without such knowledge one achieves the opposite result. These are general suggestions for teaching and learning.

Book of Rites, chapter 16

HE WHO learns daily yet knows what he lacks, and does not forget what he has learnt over the months, may be called a true lover of learning.

Analects 19:5

THE SON of a tailor learns naturally how to mend fur coats; the son of a good craftsman learns naturally how to make a bamboo basket; to tame a horse one puts it behind the carriage. A gentleman can learn from these three things the right method of education.

Book of Rites, chapter 16

A DEVELOPING
TRADITION

In this section, we look at the different ways in which Japanese Confucianism reacted to the heritage received from China. Our first example, Kaibara Ekken, who lived from 1630 to 1714, was a pioneer in bringing Confucianism to the new Japanese society of his age; his approach is conspicuously practical and down to earth.

THE *FOUR BOOKS* should be recited every day at the rate of one hundred characters repeated one hundred times, reading and writing from memory...The *Analects* is 12,700 characters, the *Mencius* 34,685 characters, the *Great Learning,* text and commentary together, 1,851 characters, and the *Doctrine of the Mean* 3,568 characters. The *Four Books* together come to 52,804 characters. If one reads and commits them to memory at the rate of 100 characters a day, the total number of days will come to 528. At seventeen months and eighteen days, in less than a year and a half the task will be complete. If you resolve the matter promptly, this is how it will be; there is no better method of study than this. It is easy to work at, yet the outcome will be outstandingly good. When we were younger, through ignorance of this excellent method, we wasted time in vain, and now I am in my eighties and conscious of the passing of the years, even though at length I have come to realise the way to study, I regret that waste very deeply.

Moreover, if one takes the best few chapters of the *Book of Documents*, all of the *Book of Odes* and *Book of Changes*, and selects 30,000 characters of the best passages from the 99,000 of the *Book of Rites*, plus several tens of thousands from the key parts of the *Zuo Commentary*, and sets up a daily programme of reading them one hundred times, for literary studies there will be nothing like it. This is an excellent method for learning.

Kaibara Ekken, Wazoku dōjikun

It might be imagined that such a commitment to rote learning would crush all creativity. Yet this was not the case. Miura Baien, a Japanese scholar who lived from 1723 to 1789, owed a great deal to his Confucian education. But he demonstrates that the tradition did not blind the more perceptive to ways of thinking that look today remarkably scientific.

PEOPLE THESE days who are supposed to understand the natural world describe celestial phenomena and geographical patterns, and trace the movements of sun, moon, stars and planets. Sure enough, those who work at their own narrow field of knowledge, if they worry at it constantly, may reach a high level of academic sophistication, but as I have

An acolyte or guardian on a terrace in the Forest of Confucius, Qufu.

said before, that is about all. Ask them why the sun revolves around the heavens once in a year, or why the heavens revolve about the earth once in a day, or why the ecliptic is sometimes to the north and sometimes to the south, and they will turn round and say that is the way things are because that is the way things are – hardly a penetrating analysis.

Certainly there are books, but men of old wrote those books on the basis of what they saw in front of them; it is not as though the forces of nature themselves wrote the books. So those writers plainly might understand some things, yet in other respects might be stymied, just as humans can understand language, yet are stymied when it comes to the faculty of smell, wherein they are inferior to dogs and cats. Furthermore from of old those who have been capable of writing books have been a cut above the average, so it may be fine to rely on books in the first instance. Yet whether or not they were written by individuals who were able to grasp the whole natural world and internalise it, they had their prejudices, and if they did not get their evidence straight, then their books will have become the cause of conditioning.

That books may be a cause of conditioning may seem to be something of an extreme opinion, but if we take an everyday example, twins at the time when they are born together will still not have lost their natural innocence. But send one to become a Buddhist monk of one sect, and one to become a Buddhist monk of a rival sect, and let them each study for ten years with their different masters. When they meet, their opinions after ten years of conditioning will be as irreconcilable as ice and burning coals – they will maintain their opinions to the death. Even were they to try to recover the natural innocence they had at birth, how could they achieve it once more?

MIURA BAIEN, *Miura Baien shū*, '*Taga Bokkei kun ni kotauru sho*'

In a culture much more deeply influenced by Buddhism, Japanese Confucians displayed both an acute awareness of how the two traditions had become intertwined and a resolute determination to rescue Confucianism from Buddhist influence, not least in the matter of the conception of tradition itself. A leader in this respect was Itō Jinsai (1627–1705).

Y OU RAISE the question of Zen having its charts of lineages of masters and disciples, while Confucianism has charts of the transmission of the Way. And yet the Confucian transmission of the Way is less accurate than the Zen transmission from patriarch to patriarch, one directly to the other, in your opinion. My response is that charts of the transmission of the Way were created on the model of the lineage charts of recent second-rate Confucian sects. They do not represent the intention of the sages. A transmission of the type favoured by the Zen sects is making a private matter of the Way in this world, turning it into the possession of a single school. But the Way exists among men in just the same manner that the sun and moon are fixed in the heavens – anyone with eyes can see them.

ITŌ JINSAI, *Dōjimon* 3

The following passages, from a work by Dazai Shundai, who lived from 1680 to 1747, gives a final impression of the distinctive flavour of Japanese Confucianism – critical, yet passionately committed. Dazai belonged to a trend related to but distinct from that initiated by Jinsai.

Statue of Confucius at entry to the new Confucian Institute, Qufu.

FOR ANY student wishing to establish a proper attitude, there are three key words. The first is faith; the second, decisiveness; the third, effort. As for the first, it is faith in antiquity. Confucius said, 'I have faith in and love the ancient' (*Analects* 7:1), referring not to other people but to himself; the phrase means that he had faith in antiquity and loved it. This he said, though he was a sage himself, so how much more so should students of later times have faith in it! In a Buddhist book it says, 'The Buddha's teaching is a great ocean; it is by faith that we enter in' – a famous saying. This means that since the Buddha's teaching is like a great ocean, it is difficult to enter into it easily, but so long as we have faith, anyone may enter in. Though the teachings of the Buddha are far removed from ordinary human feelings, the believer may easily enter in; though the teachings of the sages are established upon ordinary human feelings, those who do not believe will not be able to enter in. Thus on the path of study faith is the first step. However much we may hear of that good path, if we do not believe, it will be of no benefit to us.

DAZAI SHUNDAI, *Seigaku Mondō*

THERE ARE, moreover, degrees of depth of faith. If one's faith is shallow, the benefit will be slight, whereas if one's faith is deep the benefit will be great. Hence in the matter of faith, deep faith is superior. That is what it means when in the *Analects* (8:13) it says 'With sincere faith he loves learning' – Yan Yuan is declared to have loved learning because he had a sincere faith. When Confucius said of him, 'I say nothing in which he does not take pleasure' (*Analects* 11:3), this was because of the sincerity of his faith in Confucius, whereas he criticised Zi Zhang as one who did not believe sincerely in the Way. The Way means the Way of the sage-kings of the past, the teachings of Confucius. We should know that it was with these teachings that the worthies of the Confucian school established a proper attitude.

DAZAI SHUNDAI, *Seigaku Mondō*

B UT IF now we turn to students of our own degenerate times, and ask what we should believe, then it is essential for students today to believe in the Way as well. Faith in itself may be misguided, by which I mean not believing in the sages of old, and having faith in latter-day teachers. Those who study the Cheng brothers and Zhu Xi have faith in them, not in Confucius. Those who study Wang Yangming (1472–1529) have faith in him, not in Confucius. Such is mistaken faith. The Cheng brothers, Zhu Xi and Wang Yangming, having all not had faith in Confucius, out of envy of the Buddhists took the Way of the ancient sage-kings and remodelled it on the Buddha's teachings, establishing mere sectarian interpretations of it. Later students moreover put their faith in the Cheng brothers, Zhu Xi and Wang Yangming, only reading the books of their particular school. They looked upon the ancient literature and institutions of Confucianism as no more than crude external indications of the Way, and on inner states as more refined and subtle, and then concentrated on abandoning the crude in favour of the subtle. This was to emulate the Buddhists in their distaste for activism and elevation of the principle of inaction.

DAZAI SHUNDAI, *Seigaku Mondō*

Formal entry to dwelling, Forest of Confucius, Qufu.

SOURCES

Analects of Confucius: Lunyu, the sayings of Confucius collected by his disciples. One of the *Four Books* (q.v.). For a translation, see e.g, Arthur Waley (ed. and trans.), *The Analects of Confucius.* London, George Allen & Unwin Ltd, 1938.

Book of Rites: Liji, a collection of accounts of rituals and other related matters going back in theory to the time of Confucius, but in the view of some modern scholars actually assembled late in the first century CE. Translated by James Legge for the series Sacred Books of the East, volumes 27 and 28, as *The Li Ki* (Oxford, Clarendon Press, 1885), with many subsequent reprints.

Book of Changes: Yijing, a manual of divination, with some later philosophical material, attributed to Confucius, attached. The current text mainly goes back to the second century BCE. The first reliable English translation was done by James Legge for the series Sacred Books of the East, volume 16, as *The Yi King* (Oxford, Clarendon Press, 1899).

Beixi ziyi: By Chen Chun, 1159–1223. A systematic interpretation of the terms used by Neo-Confucians, with a number of the author's lectures and other essays attached. For a full translation, see Wing-tsit Chan (ed. and trans.),

Neo-Confucian Terms Explained. New York, Columbia University Press, 1986.

Doctrine of the Mean: Zhong yong, one of the *Four Books* (q.v.); a short essay, originally part of the *Book of Rites* (q.v.).

Dōjimon: Answers to a Child's Questions, a work by the Japanese thinker Itō Jinsai (1627–1705). An old but still valuable work on its author is *Itō Jinsai: A philosopher, Educator and Sinologist of the Tokugawa Period*. Peking, Catholic University, 1948.

Er-Cheng Quanshu: The Complete Works of the Cheng Brothers, (including *Er-Cheng Yishu*), the Cheng brothers being Cheng Hao (1032–85) and Cheng Yi (1033–1107), pioneering Neo-Confucian theorists. Still the best introduction to their thought, and including copious illustrative translations, is A.C. Graham, *Two Chinese Philosophers*. London, Lund Humphries, 1958.

Four Books: The Analects, Mencius, Doctrine of the Mean, and Great Learning, first selected as the four key Confucian texts by Zhu Xi (cf. next entry). They were translated into Latin by the first Jesuit missionaries to China, and into English by James Legge. His versions, in their final form as contained in the first two volumes of *The Chinese Classics*

(Oxford, Clarendon Press, 1893), have been frequently republished in East Asia.

Great Learning: The Daxue, another short essay selected by Zhu Xi (1130–1200) as one of the *Four Books* (q.v.); originally it had been a section of the *Book of Rites* (q.v.). In Neo-Confucianism, the commentary on this text by Zhu Xi was particularly important. For a translation and study of Zhu Xi's reading of this text, see Daniel K. Gardiner, *Chu Hsi and the Ta-hsueh: Neo-Confucian Reflection on the Confucian Canon.* Cambridge, MA, Harvard University Press, 1986.

Kongcongzi: The Kong Family Masters. Allegedly based on the family traditions of the descendants of Confucius, but probably put together in the third century CE, the texts represent Confucianism as it had evolved by the end of antiquity in China. For a full study with translation, see Yoav Ariel (ed. and trans.), *K'ung-Ts'ung-tzu: The K'ung Family Masters' Anthology.* Princeton: Princeton University Press, 1989.

Mencius: Mengzi, a compilation of the debates and sayings of Master Meng (fourth century BCE), in which he is represented as vigorously defending the Confucian tradition against later opponents. The Penguin Classics translation by D.C. Lau, first published in 1970, has been particularly influential.

Miura Baien shū: The Works of Miura Baien (1723–89), a remarkable Japanese thinker who was particularly concerned with understanding the natural world. Our translation is from the Iwanami Bunko edition of his writings; a more complete study including a full translation of the piece excerpted is Rosemary Mercer, *Deep Words: Miura Baien's System of Natural Philosophy*. Leiden: E.J. Brill, 1991.

Seigaku Mondō: 'Questions and Answers on the Sagely Learning', by Dazai Shundai (1680–1747). The translation from this short work is based on the text in the Iwanami series Nihon Shiso Taikei volume entitled *Sorai gakuha*, which collects the important writings of the school to which Dazai belonged. Unfortunately, scholars writing in English have scarcely touched on this interesting thinker. See, however, Tetsuo Najita, *Tokugawa political writings*. Cambridge, CUP, 1998.

Wazoku dōjikun: Precepts on Japanese Customs for Children, by Kaibara Ekken (1630–1714). Our extract is taken from the printing of this brief guide on educational matters in the Japanese Iwanami Bunko series. For the author and some of his other writings, see the study by Mary Evelyn Tucker, *Moral and Spiritual Cultivation in Japanese Neo-Confucianism*. Albany, NY: State University of New York Press, 1989.

Western Inscription: 'Xi ming', a short essay by Zhang Zai (1020–77), an important contributor to Neo-Confucian thought. Wing-tsit Chan, trans. and comp. *A Source Book in Chinese Philosophy*. Princeton, Princeton University Press, 1963, pp. 497–8, provides a full translation of this piece.

Yuanshi shifan: *The Family Instructions of Yuan Cai,* who lived in the late twelfth century. A practical handbook of guidance on family life, now available with an excellent introduction in Patricia Buckley Ebrey (trans.), *Family and Property in Sung China: Yuan Ts'ai's Precepts for Social Life*. Princeton: Princeton University Press, 1984.

FURTHER READING

The following two authors can be commended for their contrasting introductory surveys of Confucianism:

Berthrong, J.H. *Transformations of the Confucian Way.* Boulder, CO, Westview Press, 1998

Yao, X. *An Introduction to Confucianism.* Cambridge, Cambridge University Press, 2000

Also consulted:

Bruce, J.P. (trans.) *The Philosophy of Human Nature by Chu Hsi* [Zhu Xi]. London, Probsthain, 1922

Chang, C. *The Development of Neo-Confucian Thought.* New York, Bookman Associates, 1957

Chen, L. *The Confucian Way: A New and Systematic Study of 'The Four Books'*, trans. Liu Shihshun from Chinese. London and New York, KPI Ltd, 1986

Dobson, W.A.C.H. (ed. and trans.) *Mencius.* Toronto: University of Toronto Press, 1963

Fung, Y. *A History of Chinese Philosophy*, trans. Derke Bodde from Chinese. Princeton, Princeton University Press, 1952

Lin, Y. (ed. and trans.) *The Wisdom of Confucius.* New York, Random House, First Modern Library Edition, 1938

Wu, J. *Clarification and Enlightenment: Essays in Comparative Philosophy*. Washington, DC, University Press of America, 1978

An acolyte or guardian on a terrace in the Forest of Confucius, Qufu.